INVESTIGATING EARTH SYSTEMS™

AN INQUIRY EARTH SCIENCE PROGRAM

INVESTIGATING EARTH IN SPACE: ASTRONOMY

Ann Benbow, Ph.D.
Mark Carpenter
Matthew Hoover
Colin Mably

Developed by the
American Geological Institute

IT's ABOUT TIME®
HERFF JONES EDUCATION DIVISION

Published by
It's About Time, Herff Jones Education Division, Armonk, NY

HERFF JONES EDUCATION DIVISION
84 Business Park Drive, Armonk, NY 10504
Phone (914) 273-2233 Fax (914) 273-2227
Toll Free (888) 698-TIME
www.Its-About-Time.com

President
Tom Laster

Director of Product Development
Barbara Zahm, Ph.D.

Project Editor
Ruta Demery

Creative Director/Design
John Nordland

Associate Editor
Jane Gardner

Creative Artwork
Dennis Falcon

Safety Reviewer
Edward Robeck, Ph.D.

Desktop Specialist
Bernardo Saravia

Technical Art
Armstrong/Burmar

Photo Research
Bernardo Saravia, Jennifer Von Holstein

Printed and bound in the United States of America

ISBN #1-58591-265-4 (Hard Cover)
ISBN #1-58591-264-6 (Soft Cover)

1 2 3 4 5 QC 09 08 07 06

The Development Team for Investigating Earth in Space: Astronomy

Ann Benbow, Ph.D. is a researcher, curriculum developer, teacher, and trainer. She is currently Director of Education, Development and Outreach at AGI. After teaching science (biology, chemistry, and Earth science) in high school, elementary school, and two-year college, she taught elementary and secondary science methods at the university level. She worked in research and development for the Education Division of the American Chemical Society for over 12 years. During that time, she directed a number of national educational grants from the National Science Foundation (NSF). Her work in the informal science arena included a period of time as managing editor of *WonderScience* magazine for children and adults, and administrator for the Parents and Children for Terrific Science mini-grant program. Dr. Benbow is currently Principal Investigator of two NSF-supported projects, has co-authored a college textbook on elementary science methods for Wadsworth Publishing, and recently published a book on improving communication techniques with adult learners. Dr. Benbow has a B.S. in Biology from St. Mary's College in Maryland, an M.Ed. in Science Education, and a Ph.D. in Curriculum and Instruction from the University of Maryland College Park.

Mark Carpenter is an Education Specialist at the American Geological Institute. After receiving a B.S. in geology from Exeter University, England he undertook a graduate degree at the University of Waterloo and Wilfrid Laurier, Canada, where he began designing geology investigations for undergraduate students and worked as an instructor. He has worked in basin hydrology in Ontario, Canada, and studied mountain geology in the Pakistan, and the Nepal Himalayas. As a designer of learning materials for AGI, he has made educational films to support teachers and is actively engaged in designing inquiry-based activities in Earth system science for middle school children in the United States.

Matthew Hoover serves as Education Specialist for the American Geological Institute, developing Earth science educational resources and curriculum programs at the middle and high school levels. He received a B.S. degree in Geology from Boston College, an M.A. degree in Environmental Policy from George Washington University and an M.Ed. in Curriculum and Instruction from George Mason University. As a certified teacher, he has taught elementary and middle school Earth, life, and physical sciences. Prior to joining AGI, he worked for NASA's GLOBE Program, coordinating teacher trainings and designing environmental science investigations and learning activities for K-12 students.

Colin Mably is a curriculum developer, designer/illustrator, educational television producer, teacher, and trainer. He currently acts as Senior Advisor for Communications to AGI. After ten years as an elementary and middle school teacher, he joined the faculty of Furzedown College of Education and later became Principal Lecturer in the School of Education at the University of East London. Leaving academia to form an educational multimedia company, he developed video-based elementary science and mathematics curricula, in the UK and the USA. He has been a key curriculum developer for several NSF-funded national curriculum projects at middle, high school, and college levels. For AGI, he directed the design and development of the IES curriculum and also training workshops for pilot and field-test teachers. He has also recently co-authored a college textbook on elementary science methods. He received certified teacher status from Oxford University Institute of Education, and an Advanced Diploma in Education from London University Institute of Education.

Project Team

Marcus Milling
Executive Director - AGI, VA

Michael Smith
Principal Investigator

Ann Benbow
Director of Education - AGI, VA

Colin Mably
Senior Advisor for Communications - AGI, VA

Matthew Smith
Project Coordinator

Fred Finley
Project Evaluator
University of Minnesota, MN

Joe Moran
American Meteorological Society

Lynn Lindow
Pilot Test Evaluator
University of Minnesota, MN

Harvey Rosenbaum
Field Test Evaluator
Montgomery School District, MD

Robert Ridky
Original Project Director
University of Maryland, MD

Chip Groat
Original Principal Investigator - University of Texas
El Paso, TX

Marilyn Suiter
Original Co-principal Investigator - AGI, VA

William Houston
Field Test Manager

Caitlin Callahan - Project Assistant

Original and Contributing Authors

Oceans
George Dawson
Florida State University, FL

Joseph F. Donoghue
Florida State University, FL

Ann Benbow
American Chemical Society

Michael Smith
American Geological Institute

Soil
Robert Ridky
University of Maryland, MD

Colin Mably - LaPlata, MD

John Southard
Massachusetts Institute of Technology, MA

Michael Smith
American Geological Institute

Fossils
Robert Gastaldo
Colby College, ME

Colin Mably - LaPlata, MD

Michael Smith
American Geological Institute

Climate and Weather
Mike Mogil
How the Weather Works, MD

Ann Benbow
American Chemical Society

Joe Moran
American Meteorological Society

Michael Smith
American Geological Institute

Energy Resources
Laurie Martin-Vermilyea
American Geological Institute

Michael Smith
American Geological Institute

Our Dynamic Planet
Michael Smith
American Geological Institute

Rocks and Landforms
Michael Smith
American Geological Institute

Water as a Resource
Ann Benbow
American Chemical Society

Michael Smith
American Geological Institute

Materials and Minerals
Mary Poulton
University of Arizona, AZ

Colin Mably - LaPlata, MD

Michael Smith
American Geological Institute

Earth in Space: Astronomy
Ann Benbow
American Geological Institute

Mark Carpenter
American Geological Institute

Matthew Hoover
American Geological Institute

Colin Mably
American Geological Institute

Advisory Board

Jane Crowder
Middle School Teacher, WA

Kerry Davidson
Louisiana Board of Regents, LA

Joseph D. Exline
Educational Consultant, VA

Louis A. Fernandez
California State University, CA

Frank Watt Ireton
National Earth Science Teachers Association, DC

LeRoy Lee
Wisconsin Academy of Sciences, Arts and Letters, WI

Donald W. Lewis
Chevron Corporation, CA

James V. O'Connor (deceased)
University of the District of Columbia, DC

Roger A. Pielke Sr.
Colorado State University, CO

Dorothy Stout
Cypress College, CA

Lois Veath
Advisory Board Chairperson
Chadron State College, NE

Field Test Teachers and Specialists

Jenny Soro; Ruby Everage
Daniel Boone Elementary

Joyce Anderson; Maureen Tucker
Burnside Scholastic Academy

Aimee Ray; Marvin Nochowitz
Haines Elementary

Nicole Hauser; Noreen Sepulveda
Healy Elementary

Roseann Pavelka; Ann Doyle
Kinzie Elementary

Katherine Lee
McCorkle Elementary

Terri Zachary; Chandra Garcia
O'Toole Elementary

Brenda Armstrong; Delores McKinney
Overton Elementary

Kathryn Doyle; Patsy Moore
Pirie Magnet Elementary

Veronica Johnson; Constance Grimm-Grason
Ray Elementary

Mary Pat Robertson; Constance Grimm-Grason
Ray Elementary

Raymond Montes; Barbara Dubielak-Wood
Reilly Elementary

Raul Bermejo; Tammy Valaveris
Columbia Explorers Academy

Kim John-Baptiste; Lillian Degand
Finkl Elementary

Marie Clouston
Peck Elementary

Facilitators

Linda Carter, Gary Morrissey, Alan Nelson
Office of Math and Science for Chicago Public Schools

IMPORTANT NOTICE

The *Investigating Earth Systems*™ series of modules is intended for use by students under the direct supervision of a qualified teacher. The experiments described in this book involve substances that may be harmful if they are misused or if the procedures described are not followed. Read cautions carefully and follow all directions. Do not use or combine any substances or materials not specifically called for in carrying out experiments. Other substances are mentioned for educational purposes only and should not be used by students unless the instructions specifically indicate.

The materials, safety information, and procedures contained in this book are believed to be reliable. This information and these procedures should serve only as a starting point for classroom or laboratory practices, and they do not purport to specify minimal legal standards or to represent the policy of the American Geological Institute. No warranty, guarantee, or representation is made by the American Geological Institute as to the accuracy or specificity of the information contained herein, and the American Geological Institute assumes no responsibility in connection therewith. The added safety information is intended to provide basic guidelines for safe practices. It cannot be assumed that all necessary warnings and precautionary measures are contained in the printed material and that other additional information and measures may not be required.

Table of Contents

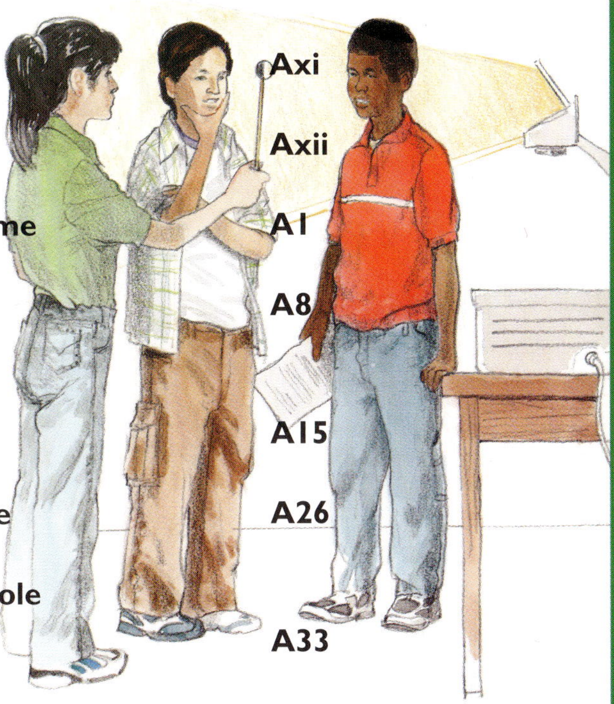

Using Investigating Earth Systems

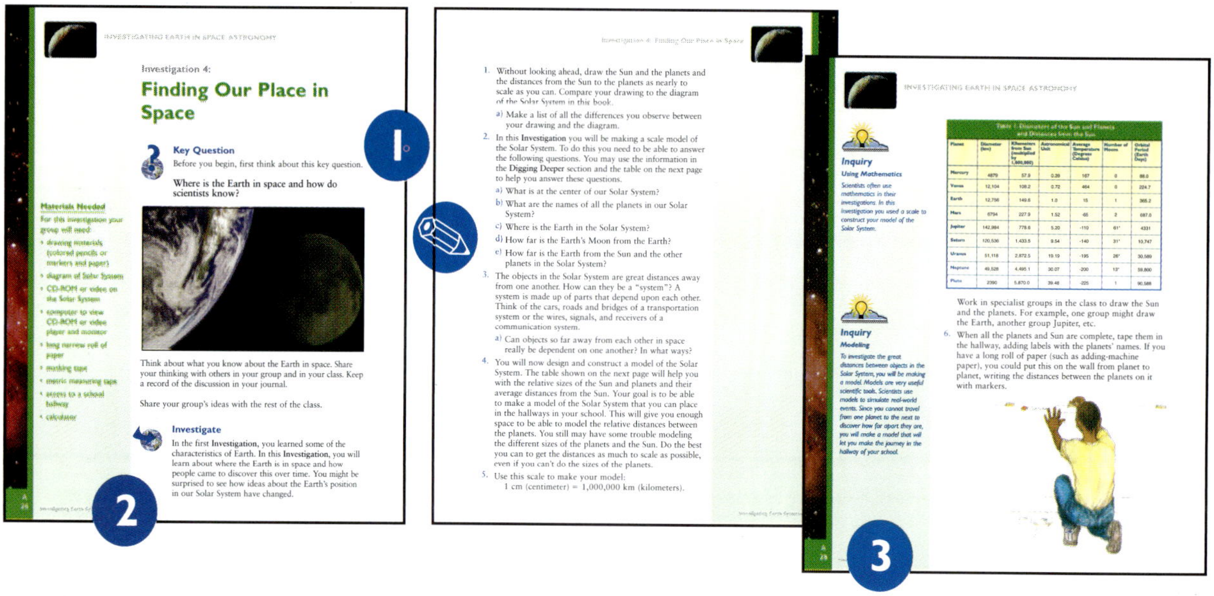

Look for the following features in this module to help you learn about the Earth System.

1. Key Question

Before you begin, you will be asked to think about the key question you will investigate. You do not need to come up with a correct answer. Instead, you will be expected to take some time to think about what you already know. You can then share your ideas with your small group and with the class.

2. Investigate

Geoscientists learn about the Earth System by doing investigations. That is exactly what you will be doing. Sometimes you will be given the procedures to follow. Other times you will need to decide what question you want to investigate and what procedure to follow.

Throughout your investigations you will keep your own journal. Your journal is like one that scientists keep when they investigate a scientific question. You can enter anything you think is important during the investigation. There will also be questions after many of the **Investigate** steps for you to answer and enter in your journal. You will also need to think about how the Earth works as a set of systems. You can write the connections you make after each investigation on your *Earth System Connection* sheet in your journal.

3. Inquiry

You will use inquiry processes to investigate and solve problems in an orderly way. Look for these reminders about the processes you are using.

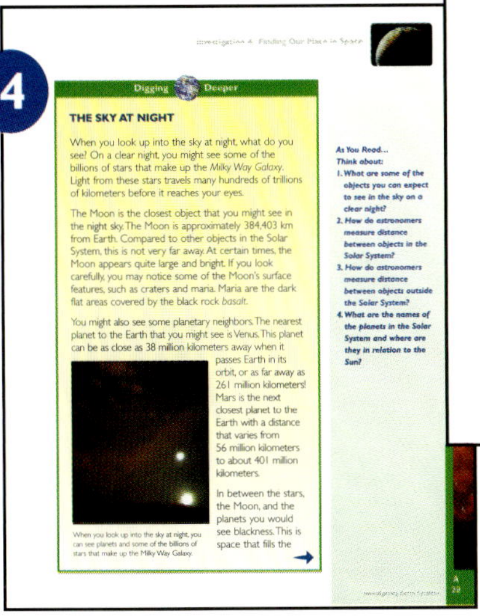
4

Investigation 4: Finding Our Place in Space

Digging Deeper

THE SKY AT NIGHT

When you look up into the sky at night, what do you see? On a clear night, you might see some of the billions of stars that make up the *Milky Way Galaxy*. Light from these stars travels many hundreds of trillions of kilometers before it reaches your eyes.

The Moon is the closest object that you might see in the night sky. The Moon is approximately 384,403 km from Earth. Compared to other objects in the Solar System, this is not very far away. At certain times, the Moon appears quite large and bright. If you look carefully, you may notice some of the Moon's surface features, such as craters and maria. Maria are the dark flat areas covered by the black rock *basalt*.

You might also see some planetary neighbors. The nearest planet to the Earth that you might see is Venus. This planet can be as close as 38 million kilometers away when it passes Earth in its orbit, or as far away as 261 million kilometers! Mars is the next closest planet to the Earth with a distance that varies from 56 million kilometers to about 401 million kilometers.

In between the stars, the Moon, and the planets you would see blackness. This is space that fills the

When you look up into the sky at night, you can see planets and some of the billions of stars that make up the Milky Way Galaxy.

As You Read...
Think about:
1. What are some of the objects you can expect to see in the sky on a clear night?
2. How do astronomers measure distance between objects in the Solar System?
3. How do astronomers measure distance between objects outside the Solar System?
4. What are the names of the planets in the Solar System and where are they in relation to the Sun?

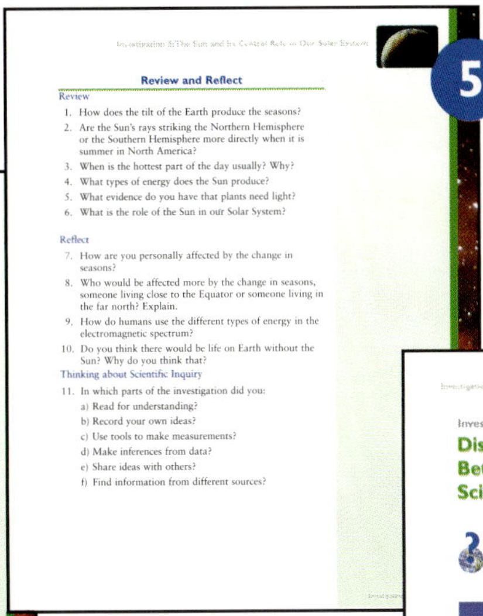
5

Investigation 5: The Sun and Its Central Role in Our Solar System

Review and Reflect

Review

1. How does the tilt of the Earth produce the seasons?
2. Are the Sun's rays striking the Northern Hemisphere or the Southern Hemisphere more directly when it is summer in North America?
3. When is the hottest part of the day usually? Why?
4. What types of energy does the Sun produce?
5. What evidence do you have that plants need light?
6. What is the role of the Sun in our Solar System?

Reflect

7. How are you personally affected by the change in seasons?
8. Who would be affected more by the change in seasons, someone living close to the Equator or someone living in the far north? Explain.
9. How do humans use the different types of energy in the electromagnetic spectrum?
10. Do you think there would be life on Earth without the Sun? Why do you think that?

Thinking about Scientific Inquiry

11. In which parts of the investigation did you:
a) Read for understanding?
b) Record your own ideas?
c) Use tools to make measurements?
d) Make inferences from data?
e) Share ideas with others?
f) Find information from different sources?

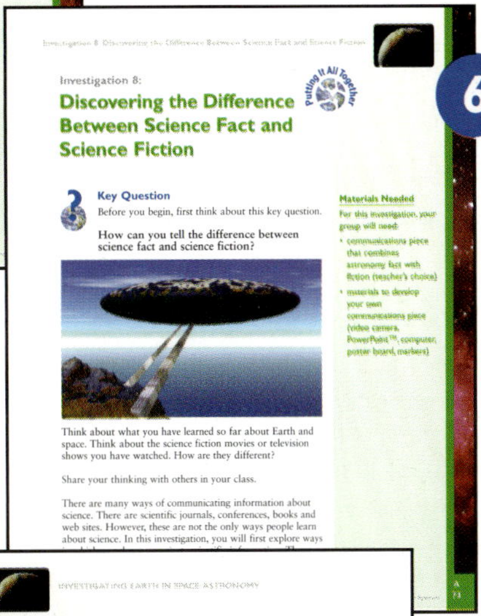
6

Investigation 8: Discovering the Difference Between Science Fact and Science Fiction

Investigation 8:
Discovering the Difference Between Science Fact and Science Fiction

Putting It All Together

Key Question

Before you begin, first think about this key question.

How can you tell the difference between science fact and science fiction?

Think about what you have learned so far about Earth and space. Think about the science fiction movies or television shows you have watched. How are they different?

Share your thinking with others in your class.

There are many ways of communicating information about science. There are scientific journals, conferences, books and web sites. However, these are not the only ways people learn about science. In this investigation, you will first explore ways

Materials Needed

For this investigation, your group will need:
- communications piece that combines astronomy fact with fiction (teacher's choice)
- materials to develop your own communications piece (video camera, PowerPoint™, computer, poster board, markers)

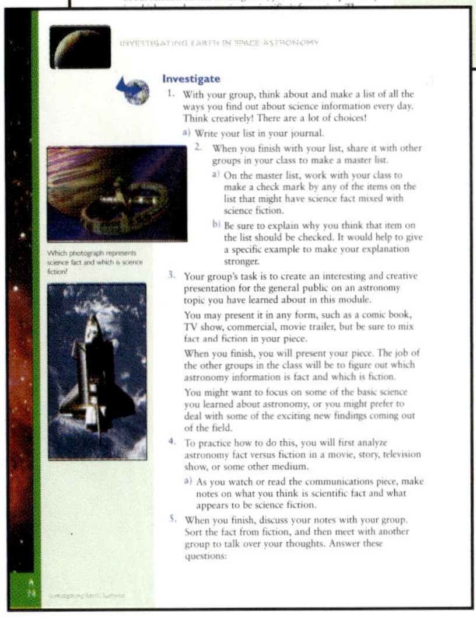

Investigating Earth in Space: Astronomy

Investigate

1. With your group, think about and make a list of all the ways you find out about science information every day. Think creatively! There are a lot of choices!
a) Write your list in your journal.
2. When you finish with your list, share it with other groups in your class to make a master list.
a) On the master list, work with your class to make a check mark by any of the items on the list that might have science fact mixed with science fiction.
b) Be sure to explain why you think that item on the list should be checked. It would help to give a specific example to make your explanation stronger.
3. Your group's task is to create an interesting and creative presentation for the general public on an astronomy topic you have learned about in this module.
You may present it in any form, such as a comic book, TV show, commercial, movie trailer, but be sure to mix fact and fiction in your piece.
When you finish, you will present your piece. The job of the other groups in the class will be to figure out which astronomy information is fact and which is fiction.
You might want to focus on some of the basic science you learned about astronomy, or you might prefer to deal with some of the exciting new findings coming out of the field.
4. To practice how to do this, you will first analyze astronomy fact versus fiction in a movie, story, television show, or some other medium.
a) As you watch or read the communications piece, make notes on what you think is scientific fact and what appears to be science fiction.
5. When you finish, discuss your notes with your group. Sort the fact from fiction, and then meet with another group to talk over your thoughts. Answer these questions:

Which photograph represents science fact and which is science fiction?

4. Digging Deeper

Scientists build on knowledge that others have discovered through investigation. In this section you can read about the insights scientists have about the question you are investigating. The questions in **As You Read** will help you focus on the information you are looking for.

5. Review and Reflect

After you have completed each investigation, you will be asked to reflect on what you have learned and how it relates to the "Big Picture" of the Earth System. You will also be asked to think about what scientific inquiry processes you used.

6. Investigation: Putting It All Together

In the last investigation of the module, you will have a chance to "put it all together." You will be asked to apply all that you have learned in the previous investigations to solve a practical problem. This module is just the beginning! You continue to learn about the Earth System every time you ask questions and make observations about the world around you.

The Earth System

The Earth System is a set of systems that work together in making the world we know. Four of these important systems are:

The Atmosphere
This part of the Earth System is made of the mixture of gases that surround the planet.

The Biosphere
This part of the Earth Systen is made of all living things including plants, animals and other organisms

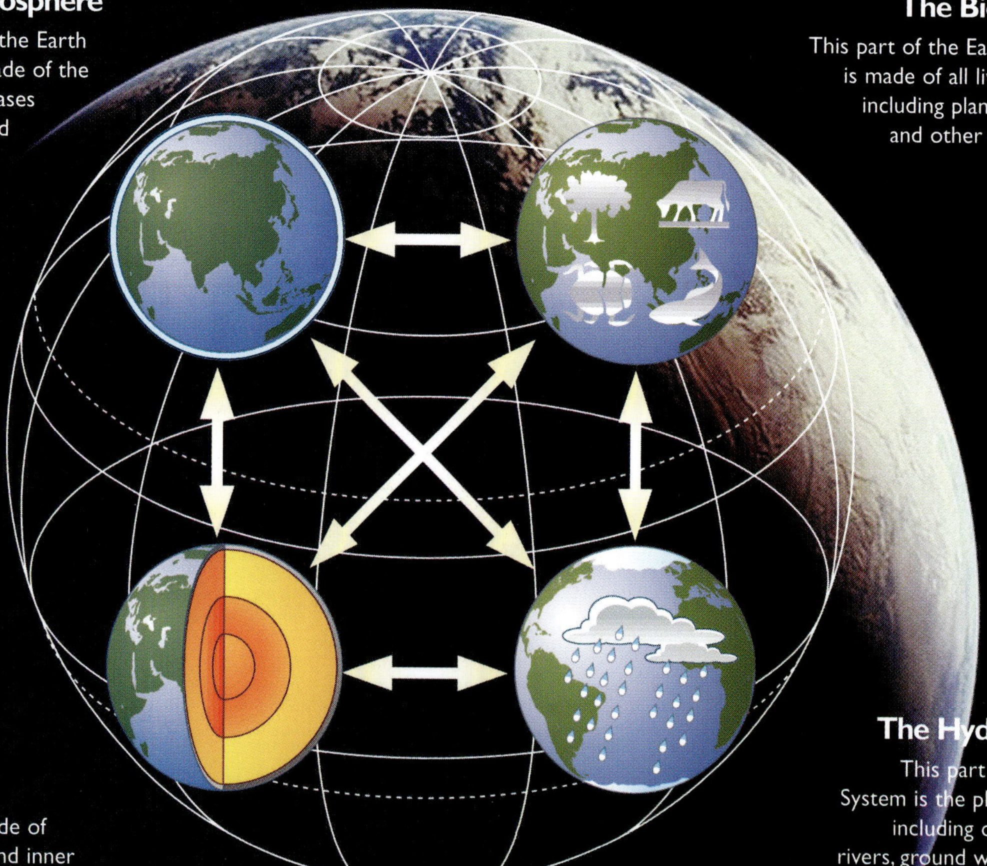

The Geosphere
This part of the Earth System is made of the crust, mantle, and inner and outer core.

The Hydrosphe
This part of the Ear System is the planet's wat including oceans, lak rivers, ground water, ice, a water vap

These systems, and others, have been working together since the Earth's beginning more than 4.6 billion years ago. They are still working, because the Earth is always changing, even though we cannot always observe these changes. Energy from within and outside the Earth leads to changes in the Earth System. Changes in any one of these systems affects the others. This is why we think of the Earth as made of interrelated systems.

During your investigations, keep the Earth System in mind. At the end of each investigation, you will be asked to think about how the things you have discovered fit with the Earth System.

To further understand the Earth System, take a look at THE BIG PICTURE shown on page 78.

Introducing Inquiry Processes

When geologists and other scientists investigate the world, they use a set of inquiry processes. Using these processes is very important. They ensure that the research is valid and reliable. In your investigations, you will use these same processes. In this way, you will become a scientist, doing what scientists do. Understanding inquiry processes will help you to investigate questions and solve problems in an orderly way. You will also use inquiry processes in high school, in college, and in your work.

During this module, you will learn when, and how, to use these inquiry processes. Use the chart below as a reference about the inquiry processes.

Inquiry Processes:	How scientists use these processes
Explore questions to answer by inquiry	Scientists usually form a question to investigate after first looking at what is known about a scientific idea. Sometimes they predict the most likely answer to a question. They base this prediction on what they already know or believe to be true.
Design an investigation	To make sure that the way they test ideas is fair, scientists think very carefully about the design of their investigations. They do this to make sure that the results will be valid and reliable.
Conduct an investigation	After scientists have designed an investigation, they conduct their tests. They observe what happens and record the results. Often, they repeat a test several times to ensure reliable results.
Collect and review data using tools	Scientists collect information (data) from their tests. Data can take many forms. Common kinds of data include numerical (numbers), verbal (words), and visual (images). To collect and manage data, scientists use tools such as computers, calculators, tables, charts, and graphs.
Use evidence to develop ideas	Evidence is very important for scientists. Just as in a court case, it is proven evidence that counts. Scientists look at the evidence other scientists have collected, as well as the evidence they have collected themselves.
Consider evidence for explanations	Finding strong evidence does not always provide the complete answer to a scientific question. Scientists look for likely explanations by studying patterns and relationships within the evidence.
Seek alternative explanations	Sometimes, the evidence available is not clear or can be interpreted in other ways. If this is so, scientists look for different ways of explaining the evidence. This may lead to a new idea or question to investigate.
Show evidence & reasons to others	Scientists communicate their findings to other scientists. Other scientists may then try to repeat the investigation to validate the results.
Use mathematics for science inquiry	Scientists use mathematics in their investigations. Accurate measurement, with suitable units, is very important for both collecting and analyzing data. Data often consist of numbers and calculations.

Introducing Earth in Space: Astronomy

Have you ever looked at the stars and wondered how far away they were?

Have you noticed changes in the way the Moon looks?

Did you ever wonder what it would be like to travel in space?

Have you ever looked through a telescope?

Why is Astronomy Important?

Astronomy is the study of the Moon, stars, and other objects in space. It is important because it helps you understand how the Earth system works within the Solar System and beyond. It is an amazing science because it explores space from its tiny specks of dust to its huge clusters of stars. From the beginning, humans have been fascinated by the objects in the night sky. At first, it seemed like there was just the Moon and stars, but early astronomers began to notice other objects, too. They noticed comets and meteors (called "falling stars" by early observers) moving across the skies. They also discovered that the planets were brighter and moved differently from the stars. One of the most important advances in the history of astronomy was the invention of the telescope in the 1600s. A telescope could magnify the objects in the sky. The more complex telescopes became, the more discoveries astronomers were able to make. The planet Mars looked red. Saturn had rings around it, but why? The telescope created even more questions than it answered, but astronomers kept seeking the answers. Astronomy is important because it helps you understand the universe within which Earth exists.

What Will You Investigate?

To help you understand more about the science of astronomy, you will be conducting research. Your research will include hands-on investigations. You will also make and study models. Here are some of the things you will investigate:

- what characteristics the planet Earth has
- where Earth is in our Solar System
- what other planets and objects are in the Solar System
- what the similarities and differences are between the planets
- the role of the Sun in the Solar System
- how the different parts of the Solar System relate to one another
- the objects outside our Solar System
- the life cycle of stars
- how people have studied the universe over time
- the latest theories about how our universe formed.

You will need to practice your problem-solving skills and become an accurate observer and recorder. You will also need to be creative in researching information about the universe.

In the last **Investigation** you will have a chance to apply all that you learned about Earth and space. You will create an exciting piece of communication on an astronomy topic you have learned about in this module.

Investigation 1:

There's No Place Like Home

Key Question

Before you begin, first think about this key question.

What characteristics does the planet Earth have and how do scientists know this?

A look at Earth from space.

Think about what you already know about the Earth. Write down two things that you feel confident you know about the Earth as a planet. You may want to draw a picture as well. Then, write down how you think scientists have discovered these things about the Earth. What tools or methods do you think they have used?

When you finish, share your ideas with other students in your group. Make a group list of what you know and what questions you would like to investigate about the Earth and how scientists study the Earth. Keep this list for later in your investigation.

Materials Needed

For this investigation your group will need:

- colored pencils or markers and blank paper
- diagram of the Earth, showing the different layers
- relief map or globe of the Earth
- 5" x 8" index cards
- computer with Internet access, if possible

Investigate

1. Use the ideas and drawings about the Earth that your group members have already finished. Work together to draw two sketches.
   a) One sketch should show the Earth as if you were looking down on it from space. Try to show as many features of the planet as you can. Label any features (continents, oceans, mountains, etc.) that you know.

Inquiry

Making Diagrams

Sometimes the best way to show the results of a scientific investigation is by drawing a diagram. Complicated concepts can often be illustrated more easily than they can be explained in words. The diagram should be labeled.

b) The second sketch should show what you and your other group members think that the inside of the Earth looks like. Imagine that you could cut the Earth in half. Do your best to show what it might look like beneath the surface. Label your sketch with descriptions of the different parts you have drawn. If you know the names of any of the Earth's layers, label these, but don't worry if you don't know this yet.

2. Label your drawings with your group's initials. Then post them up in a gallery around the room. Taking your journals, go on a "tour" around the gallery.

   a) Write down ideas that other groups have about the outside and inside of the planet.

3. When you finish the tour, talk about these ideas in your group. What ideas did you get from the other groups?

4. Now, look at the world map or globe your teacher will provide. Also look at the diagram of the inside of the Earth in the **Digging Deeper** section.

   a) How are your drawings (and those of your classmates) similar to or different from these maps and diagrams?

   b) What surprised you about the maps and diagrams?

   c) Use this new information to make your drawings as accurate as possible.

5. Next make a "Planet Card" (like a baseball card) about the Earth. Draw a picture of the Earth on one side of a 5" x 8" card and put important information that you have learned about the Earth on the back. You might include information on the following topics:

- What the surface of the Earth is like.
- What the interior of the Earth is like.

As you continue reading this chapter and learn more about the Earth, you can add to the Planet Card. You can also make other Planet Cards as you learn about the other planets in the Solar System. These cards can be used as a review tool later.

6. At the beginning of this **Investigation**, you also wrote down your thoughts about how scientists found out about the characteristics of the Earth. Share your thoughts with your group. Then, as a group, choose one question that you wish to investigate further. Possible topics may include, but are not limited to, the following:
   - How did scientists discover the composition of Earth's atmosphere?
   - How do scientists know what the inside of Earth is like?
   - How deep are the oceans and how can you be sure about this?
   - How high are the highest mountain ranges on Earth?
   - What is the deepest spot in the ocean?
   - Where is the highest mountain?
7. Your class will go to the library or computer center in your school to research these topics. Be sure to ask for help from your teacher if you are having difficulty finding the information you are looking for.
8. When you finish your research, think of a way that you can present your information so that your classmates find it interesting and informative. You might want to use a PowerPoint™ presentation, an overhead transparency, a poster, photographs, or even some tools.

   a) Prepare your group's presentation.
9. Make your presentation, being sure to answer any questions from your classmates.

   a) As other people are presenting, refer to your original ideas about the Earth. Add information as you discover it. Save all this information for later investigations.

Inquiry

Scientific Questions

Science inquiry starts with a question. Scientists take what they already know about a topic, then form a question to investigate further. The question and its investigation are designed to expand their understanding of the topic. You are doing the same in this investigation.

Digging Deeper

EARTH, A CONSTANTLY CHANGING PLANET

As You Read...
Think about:
1. ***What are the layers of the Earth?***
2. ***What are the Earth's systems?***

Earth Systems

The Earth has many features and parts that work together in important ways. One way to study the Earth is to look at its different parts and understand how they are connected. With this information, you can begin to understand how the planet works and how it is always changing. Parts of the Earth that work together are known as systems. Planet Earth has four main systems: the atmosphere, the biosphere, the hydrosphere, and the geosphere.

Earth as viewed from space. Which parts of the Earth systems can you see in this photo?

Atmosphere

The picture shows Earth as viewed from space. Notice the clouds that surround the planet. They are part of an envelope of gases, called the atmosphere, that surround the Earth. When you look up into the sky from the Earth's surface, you are looking into the Earth's *atmosphere*. The gases in the atmosphere play an important role in all the Earth systems. For example, 21% of the Earth's atmosphere is oxygen. Many organisms (living things) need the oxygen in the air to live. Another important gas in the atmosphere, carbon dioxide, is used by plants to make food. Ozone is a naturally occurring gas found in a layer of the atmosphere called the stratosphere. At this level, ozone protects life on Earth from harmful energy given off by the Sun. Finally, the swirling cloud layer that you see in the photograph is condensed water vapor. This water vapor plays an important role in Earth's weather systems.

Biosphere

The Earth supports millions of different types of living organisms that make up part of the Earth's *biosphere*. Organisms survive in many places, from high atop mountains to the extreme environments of the deep ocean floor. Some live on land surfaces, while others live below thousands of meters of glacial ice. Many organisms that once lived on the Earth no longer exist. They could not adjust when conditions such as climate and food supplies changed drastically. Fossils in ancient rocks are evidence that these organisms once did live on the Earth.

Hydrosphere

Water covers nearly 71% of the Earth's surface. The part of the Earth that contains water is known as the *hydrosphere*. Most of the water on the Earth's surface is in the oceans. Oceans are found in basins that are huge depressions in the Earth's surface. Water can be found on the Earth's land surface as streams, rivers, ponds, and lakes. Water exists underground in soil and rocks. Water in the form of vapor (gas) is an important part of the Earth's atmosphere. Water is also in the cells of every living thing on the Earth.

This image shows a massive phytoplankton bloom off the coast of Tasmania. Phytoplankton are part of the Earth's biosphere.

Geosphere

The Earth is made of layers of rock, which together make up the *geosphere*. A relatively thin layer of solid rock called the crust covers the Earth's surface. The crust has a wide variety of shapes. In some places it takes the shape of hills, mountains, slopes, or canyons. In other places it takes the shape of flatlands, shorelines, or even meteorite craters. The shape of the land is always changing. One reason for these changes is that the

The shape of Earth's crust is always changing. This image shows the mountains and valleys of the Himalaya Mountains.

Earth's massive continents are constantly being moved by processes deep within the Earth. Many of these processes occur in the part of the geosphere that lies beneath the crust. This part is called the mantle. The rocks in the mantle are continuously being squeezed, deformed, and moved in different directions. Sometimes the rocks of the crust move upward to form mountain ranges. Mountain ranges can even be found beneath the oceans and are called mid-ocean ridges.

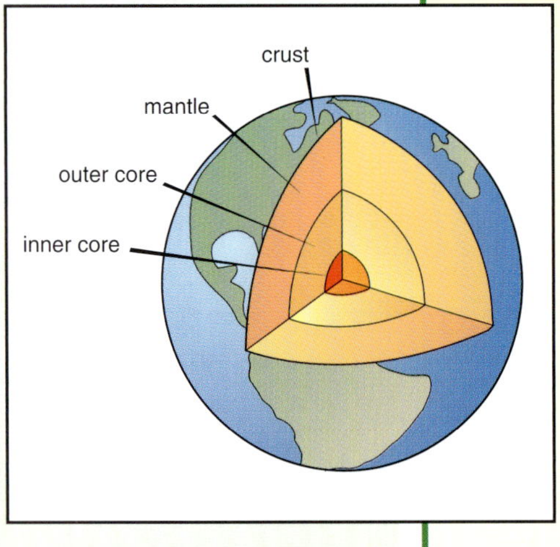

Processes deep within the Earth's interior change the shape of the landscape.

Deep beneath the Earth's mantle are two other layers: the outer core and the inner core. Both the inner and outer cores of the Earth are made mostly of iron. The inner core is solid and the outer core is liquid. These four layers – the crust, mantle, outer core, and inner core – make up Earth's geosphere.

Examining the Earth's systems provides an explanation for many of the most important features of how planet Earth works. Scientists use this knowledge when they study other planets. They compare the Earth's systems to the systems of other planets to understand how those planets work. The more they know about the Earth, the more they can learn about the other planets in the Solar System.

Review and Reflect

Review

1. What questions about the inside and outside of the Earth were you able to answer through this investigation?
2. What questions about how scientists know about the Earth were you able to answer?

Reflect

3. What ideas about the inside and outside of the Earth surprised you the most?
4. What ideas about how scientists learn about the Earth were most interesting to you? Why were they interesting?

Thinking about the Earth System

5. What are the four main systems of Earth?
6. Describe two ways that the atmosphere and biosphere are connected. Remember to write any connections you find on the *Earth System Connection* sheet.
7. How do Earth's systems help scientists study other planets?

Thinking about Scientific Inquiry

8. In which parts of the investigation did you:
   a) Ask your own questions?
   b) Record your own ideas?
   c) Revise your ideas?
   d) Use your imagination?
   e) Share ideas with others?
   f) Find information from different sources?
   g) Pull your information together to make a presentation?

Investigation 2:

The Earth's Moon

Key Question

Before you begin, first think about this key question.

What are the features of the Moon?

Share what you know about what the Moon looks like. Keep a record of your ideas in your journal.

Share your group's ideas with the rest of the class.

The universe is so vast that it is a very difficult job to study all its parts in depth. Scientists can start with the Earth, as you did in this module. From there, one method of learning more about the universe might be to investigate Earth's nearest neighbor, the Moon. Another method might be to study the object on which we depend the most for energy, the Sun. Scientists also study the relationships among Earth, Moon, and Sun.

Investigation 2 will get you started by focusing on the Moon.

Materials Needed

For Station 1 your group will need:

- Moon map
- tape (optional)
- Learning Station materials (poster board, markers, blank paper, tape, stapler)

Investigate

Your class will work in specialist groups to study the Moon. Your group will then set up Learning Stations for other class members.

Moon Station 1: Moon's Features

1. Spread out the Moon map (or tape it up) so that you can see all the information on the map. Observe the main types of features on the Moon.

2. Try to answer all the following questions about the Moon map. You can use this information in your Learning Station.

   a) What differences do you observe between how the two sides of the Moon look on the map? How could you explain these differences?

   b) What are the Moon's maria? How might they have formed?

   c) How do you think the craters formed on the Moon?

   d) Do you see any evidence that there once might have been water on the Moon? Do you see evidence that there once might have been life on the Moon? Explain your answer.

   e) How does the Moon's surface compare to the Earth's? (Look at a relief map of the Earth, or a globe.)

3. When you have finished studying the Moon map and answering the questions, think about how you could build a Learning Station to help others in your class learn more about the Moon's features.

   a) Record your plan and show it to your teacher.

Moon Station 2: Moon Phases

Materials Needed

For Station 2 your group will need:

- Moon-phase diagram
- strong lamps or flashlights
- Ping-Pong® ball
- pencil
- tape
- overhead projector (optional)
- Learning Station materials (poster board, colored pencils, blank paper, tape, stapler)
- tennis ball

1. Study the Moon-phase diagram carefully. How does the Moon appear to change, as you observe it from the Earth, over the course of a month? How could you explain this, thinking about the relationships among the Moon, the Earth, and the Sun? (You might want to look at a diagram of the Solar System.)

2. Now, look over the materials you can use to make a model of how the Moon appears to change shape. Think about these questions before you make your model:

   a) What object(s) do you have in your materials set that could represent the Sun? The Earth? The Moon?

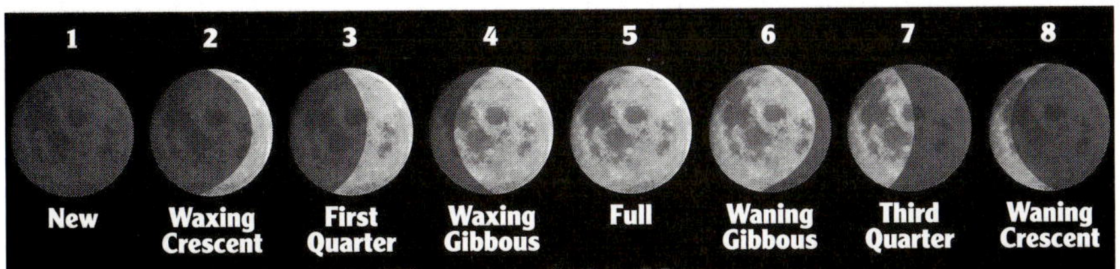

Phases of the Moon

b) Which objects would you have to move and which will you keep still?

c) How might you move those objects to show how the Earth and the Moon move?

3. You might find it useful to draw a diagram of the Sun/Earth/Moon system before building your model.

   a) Draw a diagram of your model and submit it to your teacher for approval. Use the model in your Learning Station.

Materials Needed

For Station 3 your group will need:

- Moon map
- deep metal or plastic container (such as a rectangular cake pan or storage bin)
- flour
- index card
- metric ruler
- meter stick
- small objects of various sizes and shapes (golf ball, wooden block, rock, etc.)
- Learning Station materials (poster board, colored pencils, blank paper, tape, stapler)

Moon Station 3: Moon Craters (optional)

1. Study the Moon map carefully. Note its features, particularly the craters (depressions).

   a) What are the characteristics of the craters (shape, depth, special features)?

   b) How do you think they formed?

   c) What shape and type of object most likely formed the craters?

2. Make a model of how craters formed. Fill the pan to a depth of 2.5 cm (1") with flour. This will represent the Moon's surface before it was cratered. Now, think about how you can use the collection of objects (ball, block, etc.) to make similar craters in the flour.

   a) When you have a plan, write it down and submit it to your teacher for approval.

3. Test out your plan.

   a) Be sure to record what happens and what the craters look like. You might also want to measure both the objects and the craters they form.

   b) How do the craters you made in the flour compare to the Moon's craters on the Moon map? How are they different?

   c) What object was the most likely shape to have made the craters? What evidence do you have for that?

4. When you have finished working with your crater model, figure out how you can design and build a Learning Station to help others understand how the Moon's craters were formed.

Inquiry

Sharing Findings

An important part of science inquiry is sharing the results with others. Scientists do this whenever they think that they have discovered interesting and important information. This is called disseminating research findings. In this investigation you are sharing your findings with other groups.

Building and Visiting the Learning Stations

1. After your teacher has approved your plans, prepare your Learning Station. Make sure it includes the following:
   - name of your station (Example: Moon Phases)
   - objective(s) for the station (Example: This station is designed to help visitors understand how the phases of the Moon change.)
   - materials for other groups to do part of the investigation at the station (Example: maps, models, diagrams)
   - procedure for the investigation (guidelines for how to do the investigation)
   - two questions for groups to answer or two tasks to perform to check their understanding (Example: Draw and label three phases of the Moon.)
   - scientific explanation of the important concepts for the station. (Example: A new moon occurs when . . .)

   You might find it useful to have explanation handouts to give to visitors to your center.
2. When all the Learning Stations are set up, your teacher will work with you to organize group visits to all stations. You will need to take your journals with you to record your answers to the questions at each station. Your journal will also help organize any handouts other groups may have prepared for you to take away. When you finish each station, be sure to set it back up as you found it so that other groups have the same experience you did.

   a) Answer the questions for each station in your journal.
3. When everyone finishes all the Learning Stations, have a whole-class discussion about what you learned from each station. Check your understanding of the key ideas from each station with other groups and with your teacher. Write down other questions about the Moon that you can investigate on your own later on.

As You Read...
Think about:
1. *Why does the Moon look different from Earth during the lunar cycle?*
2. *When does the new Moon occur?*
3. *When does the full Moon occur?*

Digging Deeper

THE LUNAR CYCLE

As you discovered in this investigation, the Moon's appearance changes during its orbit around the Earth. This series of phases is called the *lunar cycle*. You can only see the Moon when sunlight is reflected from its surface. The same side of the Moon always faces the Earth. As the Moon orbits the Earth, the angle between the Sun, the Earth, and the Moon changes. As this angle increases, you can see more of the Moon. Scientists can predict lunar cycles because the directions and speeds of the orbits of the Earth and Moon are very well understood.

Lunar phases depend on how the Earth, Moon, and Sun are positioned relative to one another. When the Moon is located between the Earth and the Sun, the side of the Moon that is illuminated is the side facing away from the Earth so you do not see the Moon.

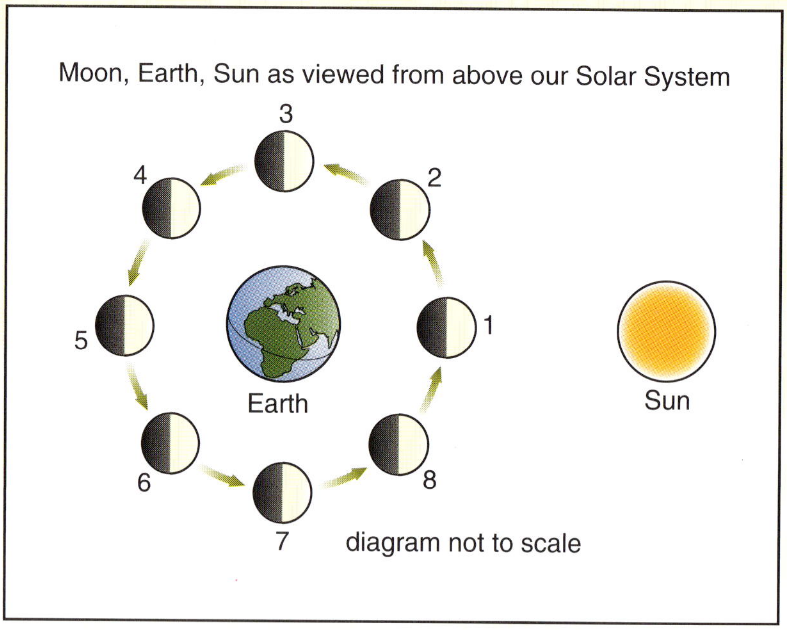

The relative positions of the Earth, Moon, and Sun determine the lunar phases.

This phase is called the *new* Moon. During the first half of the lunar cycle, you see a little more of the illuminated Moon each time it rises. When the Earth, the Moon, and the Sun are in the same plane and nearly in a line, you see either a new Moon or a *full* Moon.

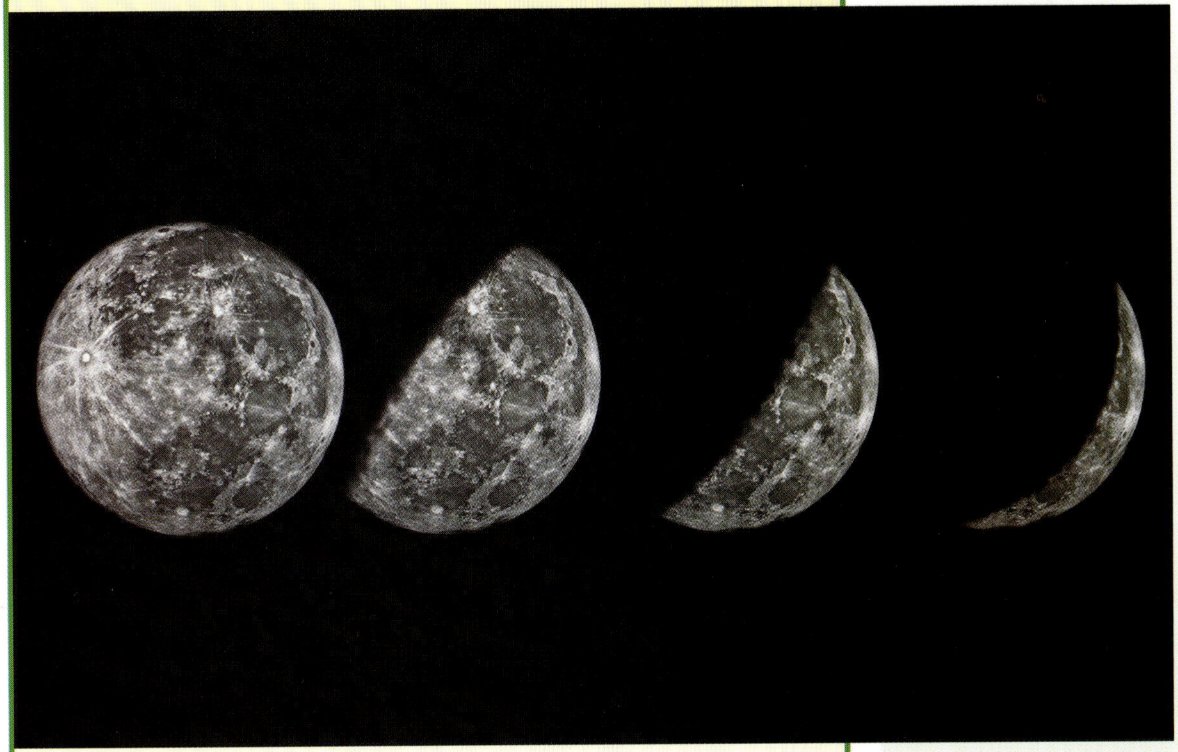

The cycle of lunar phases takes about 29.5 days to complete. After a new Moon, you gradually see more and more of the Moon until, about two weeks after the new Moon, a full moon appears in the sky. At this point, the entire visible side of the Moon is illuminated by the Sun. Over the two weeks that follow, you see less and less of the Moon until it is a new Moon again.

Review and Reflect

Review

1. Describe the main features of the Moon.
2. How can scientists predict lunar cycles?

Reflect

3. Explain why the lunar cycle is called a cycle.

Thinking about Earth System

4. How can the craters on the Moon help scientists better understand the geosphere?

Thinking about Scientific Inquiry

5. How did you use modeling in this investigation?
6. Why do you think sharing findings is an important process in scientific inquiry?

Investigation 3:

The Relationship between the Earth and Its Moon

Key Question

Before you begin, first think about this key question.

What is the relationship between the Earth and its Moon?

Share what you know about the relationship between the Earth and the Moon with others in your group. Keep a record of your ideas in your journal.

Share your group's ideas with the rest of the class.

Investigate

GravLab

The purpose of this **Investigation** is to help you understand how the force of gravity works on the Earth. It will also get you to begin thinking about the role of gravity in the Solar System and beyond. As you go through each part of the **Investigation**, think about how you are building your understanding of gravity.

1. Think about the following question: What is gravity? Talk about this with other members of your group. Here are some questions to think about during your discussion:
   - How high can you jump off the ground? What happens to you when you get to the top of your jump?

- What happens when you throw a ball into the air? How can you explain this?
- Think about any rockets you have seen on television taking astronauts into space. Why do they need so much power to get off the launch pad?
- Think about pictures of astronauts in space capsules. What is unusual about the way they move around? Why do you think this is so?

a) When you finish the discussion, write down a whole-group explanation of what you think gravity is. Do your best to agree as much as possible, but it is all right if people have different ideas at this point.

2. When you feel comfortable with your explanation, share it with the rest of the class to see what ideas other groups can add to yours. Your teacher will record the class's definition of gravity on the board or on chart paper.

   a) Record the class's definition in your journal.

You will now work with your group to investigate gravity in a number of ways. When you finish, you will revisit your class definition of gravity to see how it might need to change.

Mini-Investigation A: Gravity on the Moon

1. Look over the information in the table on the next page for this **Mini-Investigation**. It shows how much common objects weigh on Earth and how much they would weigh on the Moon.

   a) Write a sentence that explains the relationship between the weight of an object on Earth and the weight of the same object on the Moon. You do not have to use an exact number, just write a description of how the weights compare.

2. When you have thought about the relationship, check with another group to see what they have discovered. Talk this over as a class with the help of your teacher. Write your answers to the following questions:

Table: Weight of Objects on Earth and on the Moon		
Object	**Weight on Earth (kg)**	**Weight on the Moon (kg)**
Adult male African elephant	6800	1134
Pair of adult man's tennis shoes, size 9	1.2	0.2
Gallon of paint	6.6	1.1
3-L tin of cooking oil	3.0	0.5

a) Why do you think there is this relationship? Think about the size of the Earth compared to the size of the Moon. Does that help?

b) As a group, write one sentence explaining what you think the relationship is between gravity on the Moon and gravity on the Earth.

Mini-Investigation B: You're on the Moon! Now, Jump!

In this part of the **Investigation**, you will be figuring out how far you could jump if you were on the Moon. Think about **Mini-Investigation A** and the relationship you discovered between the gravity on the Earth and on the Moon. Now, imagine how that might affect how far you could jump on the Moon.

Materials Needed

For this part of the investigation your group will need:

- masking tape
- measuring tape (metric)
- calculator

1. To get a better idea of this, first see how far you can jump from a standing position on the Earth.

a) Make a data table for your group. The table should hold the following information for each student in the group: distance jumped on Earth, estimated distance on the Moon, estimated distance on Jupiter.

2. Take turns being *Jumper*, *Measurer*, and *Recorder*. Follow these steps:
   - In a hallway or the gym, use masking tape to mark a starting line.
   - *Jumper 1* stands with toes on the starting line and jumps as far as possible.
   - *Measurer 1* holds the end of the measuring tape on the starting line.
   - *Measurer 2* pulls the tape to where the Jumper lands and puts a second piece of masking tape on the floor.
   - *Measurer 2* records the Jumper's initials and length of jump in centimeters on the masking tape at the end of the jump.
   - The *Recorder* records the initials and distance in the data table for the group. The *Recorder* should also be on hand to steady the *Jumper* so that he or she doesn't fall at the end of the jump.
   - After *Jumper 1* jumps, everyone rotates roles so that all group members get a chance to jump.

3. Remember the relationship between the weight of objects on Earth and the same objects on the Moon. To find the weight of an object on the Moon, you can multiply the weight of that object on the Earth by 0.1667.

   For example:

   The weight of an elephant on Earth is 6800 kg.

   The weight of the elephant on the Moon is $6800\ \text{kg} \times 0.1667 = 1133.56\ \text{kg}$ or about 1134 kg.

   Use this procedure to determine how far each person could jump on the Moon.

   a) Place this information in the data table.

4. Measure these distances for each *Jumper* on the floor. Mark each distance with a new piece of masking tape with initials and the new distance in centimeters. Label each of these tape pieces with MJ (Moon Jump).

Inquiry

Using Mathematics

Mathematics is often used in science. In this investigation you began by comparing the weight of an object on Earth to the weight of the object on the Moon. Then you used the mathematical relationship to calculate how far you can jump on the Moon.

5. Take it one step further and think about this. The planet Jupiter has a gravitational pull that is about $2\frac{1}{2}$ (2.5) times greater than that of the Earth. How far could each of you jump on Jupiter?
   a) Do the calculations and place this information in the data table.
6. Measure these distances on the floor and make tape markers for this as well. Label each JJ (Jupiter Jump).

Mini-Investigation C: Our Moon and the Earth's Tides

In this last part of the GravLab, you will pull together what you know about the Moon and gravity to explore a major effect that the Moon has on the Earth.

1. Look at the tide table on the following pages. This table shows the level of the ocean tides during August 2004. It also shows the phases of the Moon for that same month.
2. Review what you learned in the previous investigation about the phases of the Moon and what you now know about gravity. Now, look carefully at the data in the table. Talk about the following questions. First talk with your group and then with the rest of the class. Then answer the questions in your journal.
   a) What do you think is the relationship (if any) between the tides and the phases of the Moon?
   b) How might you explain this relationship knowing what you know about the Earth, the Moon, and the pull of gravity?

Sharing and Discussing Your Findings

1. When you finish all of the GravLab, summarize what your group has learned about gravity in several clear and complete sentences.
   a) Record these sentences in your journal.
2. When you have written them in your journal, compare them to the whole-class definition of gravity.
   a) Do you need to change anything about the class definition, or add to it? Work as a class, with the help of your teacher, to come up with as complete and accurate a definition as possible. Record this in your jounal.

Inquiry

Using Data Tables as Scientific Tools

Scientists collect and review data using tools. You may think of tools as only physical objects like telescopes and measuring tapes. However, forms in which information is gathered, stored, and presented are also tools for scientists. In this investigation you are using a tide table as a scientific tool.

Ocean City (fishing pier), Maryland 38.3267° N, 75.0833° W								
August 2004								
Day	**High**	**Low**	**High**	**Low**	**High**	**Moon**	**Sunrise**	**Sunset**
Sun 01		02:41 / -0.25 ft	08:29 / 3.50 ft	14:36 / -0.58 ft	21:03 / 4.75 ft		06:02	20:09
Mon 02		03:29 / -0.29 ft	09:22 / 3.61 ft	15:29 / -0.50 ft	21:52 / 4.53 ft		06:03	20:08
Tue 03		04:15 / -0.24 ft	10:13 / 3.68 ft	16:21 / -0.31 ft	22:39 / 4.24 ft		06:04	20:07
Wed 04		05:01 / -0.13 ft	11:02 / 3.69 ft	17:15 / -0.06 ft	23:25 / 3.87 ft		06:05	20:06
Thu 05		05:46 / 0.03 ft	11:51 / 3.65 ft	18:10 / 0.23 ft			06:06	20:05
Fri 06	00:10 / 3.48 ft	06:32 / 0.21 ft	12:42 / 3.58 ft	19:07 / 0.50 ft			06:07	20:04
Sat 07	00:58 / 3.12 ft	07:18 / 0.40 ft	13:35 / 3.50 ft	20:06 / 0.72 ft		Last Quarter	06:08	20:03
Sun 08	01:49 / 2.81 ft	08:05 / 0.57 ft	14:31 / 3.45 ft	21:06 / 0.88 ft			06:09	20:02
Mon 09	02:46 / 2.61 ft	08:54 / 0.68 ft	15:31 / 3.47 ft	22:07 / 0.96 ft			06:09	20:00
Tue 10	03:45 / 2.54 ft	09:46 / 0.73 ft	16:28 / 3.54 ft	23:08 / 0.96 ft			06:10	19:59
Wed 11	04:41 / 2.58 ft	10:39 / 0.70 ft	17:20 / 3.67 ft				06:11	19:58
Thu 12		00:00 / 0.90 ft	05:32 / 2.69 ft	11:31 / 0.61 ft	18:07 / 3.83 ft		06:12	19:57
Fri 13		00:43 / 0.79 ft	06:18 / 2.85 ft	12:20 / 0.48 ft	18:50 / 3.98 ft		06:13	19:56
Sat 14		01:21 / 0.67 ft	07:01 / 3.03 ft	13:04 / 0.34 ft	19:32 / 4.12 ft		06:14	19:54

Ocean City (fishing pier), Maryland 38.3267° N, 75.0833° W

August 2004

Sun 15		01:58 / 0.45 ft	07:44 / 3.21 ft	13:47 / 0.24 ft	29:12 / 4.21 ft	New Moon	06:15	19:53
Mon 16		02:33 / 0.42 ft	08:25 / 3.38 ft	14:28 / 0.17 ft	20:51 / 4.25 ft		06:16	19:52
Tue 17		03:08 / 0.33 ft	09:07 / 3.54 ft	15:09 / 0.16 ft	21:29 / 4.21 ft		06:16	19:50
Wed 18		03:45 / 0.28 ft	09:47 / 3.69 ft	15:52 / 0.20 ft	22:08 / 4.11 ft		06:17	19:49
Thu 19		04:22 / 0.26 ft	10:29 / 3.83 ft	16:38 / 0.29 ft	22:47 / 3.93 ft		06:18	19:48
Fri 20		05:02 / 0.28 ft	11:12 / 3.94 ft	17:28 / 0.40 ft	23:30 / 3.69 ft		06:19	19:46
Sat 21		05:45 / 0.31 ft	11:59 / 4.01 ft	18:35 / 0.52 ft			06:20	19:45
Sun 22	00:16 / 3.43 ft	06:32 / 0.36 ft	12:52 / 4.05 ft	19:23 / 0.63 ft			06:21	19:44
Mon 23	01:09 / 3.17 ft	07:25 / 0.38 ft	13:52 / 4.08 ft	20:28 / 0.69 ft		First Quarter	06:22	19:42
Tue 24	02:11 / 2.98 ft	08:24 / 0.37 ft	14:59 / 4.15 ft	21:35 / 0.67 ft			06:23	19:41
Wed 25	03:19 / 2.90 ft	09:27 / 0.30 ft	16:07 / 4.27 ft	22:43 / 0.57 ft			06:24	19:39
Thu 26	04:27 / 2.97 ft	10:33 / 0.16 ft	17:11 / 4.42 ft	23:47 / 0.39 ft			06:24	19:38
Fri 27	05:30 / 3.157 ft	11:37 / -0.04 ft	18:10 / 4.56 ft				06:25	19:36
Sat 28		00:43 / 0.18 ft	06:27 / 3.38 ft	12:37 / -0.23 ft	19:04 / 4.63 ft		06:26	19:35
Sun 29		01:33 / -0.00 ft	07:21 / 3.61 ft	13:32 / -0.37 ft	19:54 / 4.62 ft	Full Moon	06:27	19:33
Mon 30		02:18 / -0.13 ft	08:12 / 3.82 ft	14:23 / -0.41 ft	20:41 / 4.50 ft		06:28	19:32
Tue 31		03:01 / -0.17 ft	09:00 / 3.97 ft	15:12 / -0.33 ft	21:26 / 4.29 ft		06:29	19:30

As You Read…
Think about:
1. What does gravitational attraction depend on?
2. Why doesn't the Sun's gravity pull all the objects in our Solar System into the Sun?
3. How does the Moon affect the Earth's tides?

Digging Deeper

GRAVITY HOLDS THE SOLAR SYSTEM TOGETHER

It is impossible to talk about the relationships among the Earth, Moon, and Sun without first learning about gravity. Gravity is the attraction of all objects to all other objects. Gravitational attraction depends on the mass (amount of matter) of the objects and the distance between them. The greater the mass of the objects, the greater is the force. The greater the distance between the objects, the smaller is the force. You can't see gravity. As a force, it is invisible.

The Sun is very far away from the Earth (approximately 150 million kilometers), but it has tremendous mass. Because of its incredible mass, the Sun has the strongest gravity in the Solar System. As the planets orbit the Sun, gravity pulls them towards the center of the Sun. Although this pull exists, the planets do not move towards the Sun's center. This is because of their forward motion. The forward movement of each planet is balanced against the Sun's gravitational pull. As a result, the planets move constantly through their orbit just fast enough to stop them from being pulled toward the Sun.

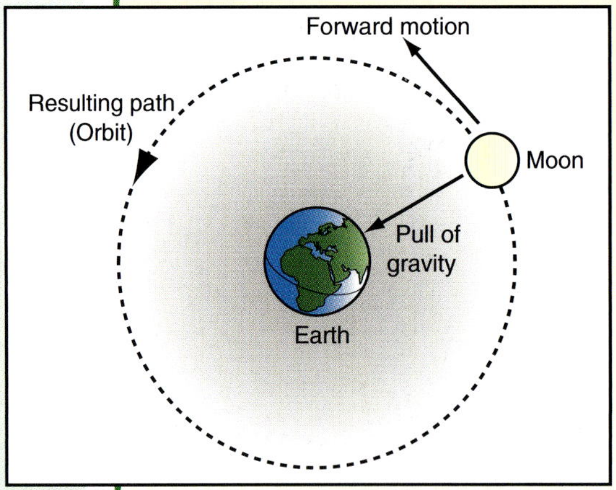

Like the planets around the Sun, the Moon's orbit around the Earth is controlled by its forward movement and the gravitational pull of the Earth.

The Sun's mass is so great that its gravity keeps the Earth (and all the other objects in the Solar System) orbiting around it. The Moon is much smaller in mass than the Earth.

However, it is relatively close to Earth and revolves around Earth. Just as the Earth's gravity keeps the Moon traveling around it, the Moon's gravity causes certain events on the Earth.

THE RISE AND FALL OF THE TIDES

The gravitational pull of the Moon is strong enough to cause the Earth's oceans to move slightly towards it. The ocean's rise in height forms a *tidal bulge* as water moves towards the Moon.

If part of the Earth's surface within the bulge has a coastline, then it will experience a *high tide*. A high tide also occurs on the opposite side of the Earth at the same time. During the Earth's 24-hour rotation, part of a coast can move into a tidal bulge. It will have a high tide inside the bulge. Then a *low tide* occurs after a coast has moved away from the bulge. Each coastal location has two high tides and two low tides daily. Together these make one *tidal cycle*.

The Sun's gravitational pull also affects the Earth's oceans. The Sun pulls the Earth's oceans in the same way as the Moon. When the Sun, the Moon, and the Earth are in alignment (during a new Moon or a full Moon), the highest high tides and the lowest low tides occur. During the half-Moon phases, the Sun and Moon pull the oceans in different directions. At this time, high tides aren't as high and low tides aren't as low.

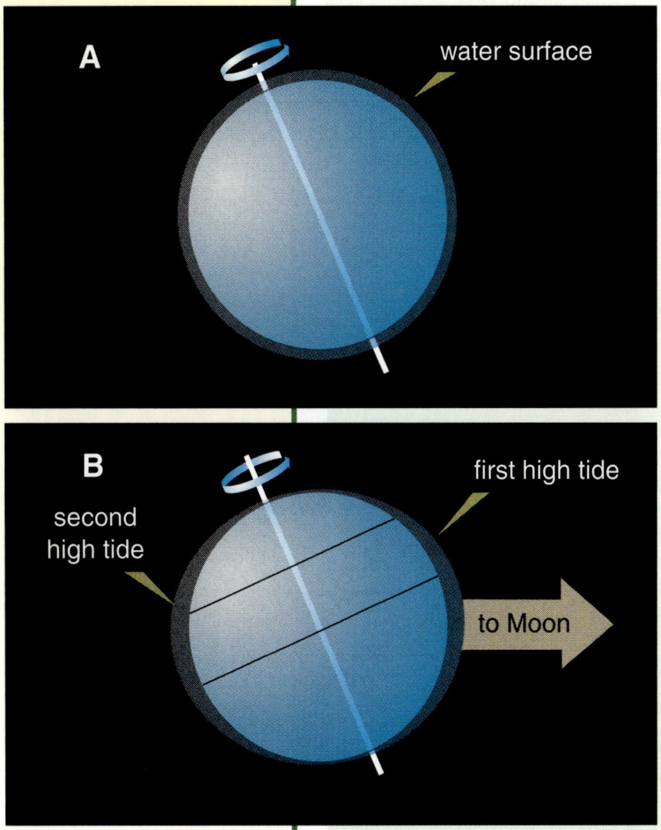

The gravitational pull of the Moon causes the Earth's oceans to form a tidal bulge.

The left image shows high tide and the right image shows low tide.

A SYSTEM IN MOTION

Despite the gigantic size of the Solar System, some of the most important processes that affect the Earth can be predicted. This is because different parts of the Solar System, such as moons or planets, move with regular cycles. Just as the Earth is a system with many parts, it is also part of a larger system involving the Sun and the Moon. Each planet and moon is also part of a larger system, called the Solar System. The key to the Solar System is the gravitational force that ties it all together.

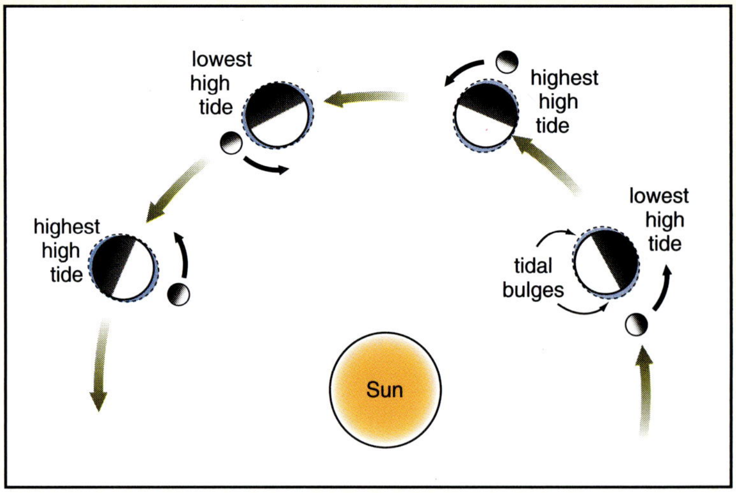

The Earth's tides are affected by the gravitational pull of both the Moon and the Sun.

Review and Reflect

Review

1. How does gravity affect our Solar System?
2. What factors affect gravity?
3. What effect does the Moon have on the Earth?
4. What effect does the Earth have on the Moon?

Reflect

5. How might motion on the Earth be different if the Earth was half its mass? Why do you think that?
6. How might motion on the Earth be different if the Earth was twice its mass? What reason do you have for that?

Thinking about the Earth System

7. How does the Moon's and Sun's gravity affect the hydrosphere?
8. How does this effect on the hydrosphere affect the other major systems. Remember to write connections, as you find them, on the *Earth System Connection* sheet.

Thinking about Scientific Inquiry

9. In which parts of the investigation did you:
   a) Make a prediction?
   b) Use tools to measure?
   c) Record your own ideas?
   d) Revise your ideas?
   e) Compare data to look for patterns and relationships?
   f) Share ideas with others?
   g) Find information from different sources?
   h) Pull your information together to make a presentation?

Investigation 4:

Finding Our Place in Space

Key Question

Before you begin, first think about this key question.

Where is the Earth in space and how do scientists know?

Think about what you know about the Earth in space. Share your thinking with others in your group and in your class. Keep a record of the discussion in your journal.

Share your group's ideas with the rest of the class.

Materials Needed

For this investigation your group will need:

- drawing materials (colored pencils or markers and paper)
- diagram of Solar System
- long narrow roll of paper
- masking tape
- metric measuring tape
- access to a school hallway
- calculator

Investigate

In the first **Investigation**, you learned some of the characteristics of Earth. In this **Investigation**, you will learn about where the Earth is in space and how people came to discover this over time. You might be surprised to see how ideas about the Earth's position in our Solar System have changed.

1. Without looking ahead, draw the Sun and the planets and the distances from the Sun to the planets as nearly to scale as you can. Compare your drawing to the diagram of the Solar System in this book.
   a) Make a list of all the differences you observe between your drawing and the diagram.
2. In this **Investigation** you will be making a scale model of the Solar System. To do this you need to be able to answer the following questions. You may use the information in the **Digging Deeper** section and the table on the next page to help you answer these questions.
   a) What is at the center of our Solar System?
   b) What are the names of all the planets in our Solar System?
   c) Where is the Earth in the Solar System?
   d) How far is the Earth's Moon from the Earth?
   e) How far is the Earth from the Sun and the other planets in the Solar System?
3. The objects in the Solar System are great distances away from one another. How can they be a "system"? A system is made up of parts that depend upon each other. Think of the cars, roads and bridges of a transportation system or the wires, signals, and receivers of a communication system.
   a) Can objects so far away from each other in space really be dependent on one another? In what ways?
4. You will now design and construct a model of the Solar System. The table shown on the next page will help you with the relative sizes of the Sun and planets and their average distances from the Sun. Your goal is to be able to make a model of the Solar System that you can place in the hallways in your school. This will give you enough space to be able to model the relative distances between the planets. You still may have some trouble modeling the different sizes of the planets and the Sun. Do the best you can to get the distances as much to scale as possible, even if you can't do the sizes of the planets.
5. Use this scale to make your model:
   1 cm (centimeter) = 1,000,000 km (kilometers).

Inquiry
Using Mathematics
Scientists often use mathematics in their investigations. In this investigation you used a scale to construct your model of the Solar System.

Table 1: Diameters of the Sun and Planets and Distances from the Sun

Planet	Diameter (km)	Kilometers from Sun (multiplied by 1,000,000)	Astronomical Unit	Average Temperature (Degrees Celsius)	Number of Moons	Orbital Period (Earth Days)
Mercury	4,879	57.9	0.39	167	0	88.0
Venus	12,104	108.2	0.72	464	0	224.7
Earth	12,756	149.6	1.0	15	1	365.2
Mars	6,794	227.9	1.52	-65	2	687.0
Jupiter	142,984	778.6	5.20	-110	61*	4,331
Saturn	120,536	1,433.5	9.54	-140	31*	10,747
Uranus	51,118	2,872.5	19.19	-195	26*	30,589
Neptune	49,528	4,495.1	30.07	-200	13*	59,800
Pluto	2,390	5,870.0	39.48	-225	1	90,588

Work in specialist groups in the class to draw the Sun and the planets. For example, one group might draw the Earth, another group Jupiter, etc.

6. When all the planets and Sun are complete, tape them in the hallway, adding labels with the planets' names. If you have a long roll of paper (such as adding-machine paper), you could put this on the wall from planet to planet, writing the distances between the planets on it with markers.

Inquiry
Modeling
To investigate the great distances between objects in the Solar System, you will be making a model. Models are very useful scientific tools. Scientists use models to simulate real-world events. Since you cannot travel from one planet to the next to discover how far apart they are, you will make a model that will let you make the journey in the hallway of your school.

Digging Deeper

THE SKY AT NIGHT

When you look up into the sky at night, what do you see? On a clear night, you might see some of the billions of stars that make up the *Milky Way Galaxy*. Light from these stars travels many hundreds of trillions of kilometers before it reaches your eyes.

The Moon is the closest object that you might see in the night sky. The Moon is approximately 384,403 km from Earth. Compared to other objects in the Solar System, this is not very far away. At certain times, the Moon appears quite large and bright. If you look carefully, you may notice some of the Moon's surface features, such as craters and maria. Maria are the dark flat areas covered by the black rock *basalt*.

You might also see some planetary neighbors. The nearest planet to the Earth that you might see is Venus. This planet can be as close as 38 million kilometers away when it passes Earth in its orbit, or as far away as 261 million kilometers! Mars is the next closest planet to the Earth with a distance that varies from 56 million kilometers to about 401 million kilometers.

When you look up into the sky at night, you can see planets and some of the billions of stars that make up the Milky Way Galaxy.

In between the stars, the Moon, and the planets you would see blackness. This is space that fills the

As You Read...
Think about:

1. What are some of the objects you can expect to see in the sky on a clear night?
2. How do astronomers measure distance between objects in the Solar System?
3. How do astronomers measure distance between objects outside the Solar System?
4. What are the names of the planets in the Solar System and where are they in relation to the Sun?

The Moon is a familiar object in the night sky. The dark areas are maria.

huge gaps between objects. It contains very little matter, except for a small amount of dust that is usually too small and far away to be seen.

EARTH'S NEAREST STELLAR NEIGHBORS

How far does light from the stars in the sky travel to reach the Earth? The Sun is the closest star to the Earth and is about 150 million kilometers away. The second nearest stellar neighbor is Proxima Centauri. Its light travels 40,000,000,000,000 km to reach the Earth!

The distances between objects in space are so huge that Earth-based units are not very useful measurements. Instead, scientists use distance units of measure that are more appropriate. For distances within the Solar System, astronomers use the astronomical unit (AU). One AU is the average distance between the Earth and the Sun or about 150 million kilometers. For distances between stars, astronomers use light-years. Light travels about 300,000 km per second. In one year it can travel 9,460,000,000,000 km. Light traveling from Proxima Centauri to the Earth takes 4.22 years. Using this measurement, you can say that Proxima Centauri is 4.22 light-years (LY) from Earth.

A composite picture of the planets in the Solar System.

MODELING THE SOLAR SYSTEM

Scientists often use models when they examine the moons, planets, stars and other objects in space. A model can be a small object that represents a larger object. Since the sizes of stars and planets are so great, scientists build small models of space systems.

These models give scientists a clearer idea of what objects are in space and how those objects interact. To

build a model, scientists must create objects and distances that are proportional to what is actually found in space. Because of the huge distances in space and the relatively small diameters of planets, making a scale model of the Solar System can take up a lot of space!

THE EARTH'S POSITION IN SPACE

The position of the Earth in space depends on its location in its orbit around the Sun. An orbit is the path and motion of one object around another object. If you look down on the Solar System from the North, with respect to Earth, each planet in the Solar System revolves around the Sun in a counter-clockwise direction. This is due to the gravitational force between the Sun and the planets. The relative position of the planets to one another depends on their positions in their orbits.

Another way to think of orbits is as a large racetrack with parallel lanes. The Sun lies near the center of the flat surface of the track. Planets race along in their lanes at different speeds and over different distances. The planets closer to the Sun on the inside lanes travel faster and over a shorter distance than the planets in lanes farther away from the Sun.

Can you imagine living on a planet that takes 248 years to orbit the Sun? This would be the case if you lived on Pluto. If you lived on Mercury, however, the closest planet to the Sun, your orbit would only take 88 days! On Earth, it takes us an average of 365.2 days to orbit the Sun.

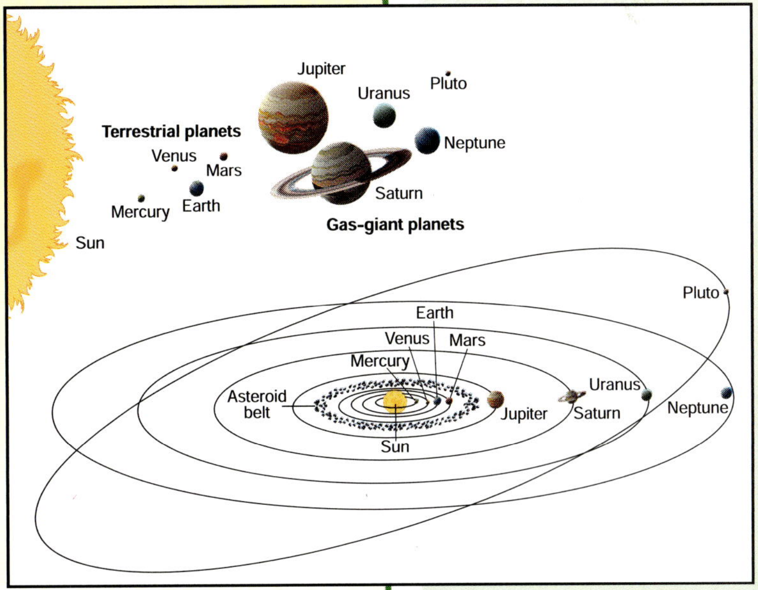

The orbits of the planets around the Sun.

Review and Reflect

Review

1. What was the most difficult part in making the model of the Solar System ? Why was this so?
2. If you traveled at the rate of 300 km/h (kilometers per hour), how long would it take you to get to Mars? To Jupiter?

Reflect

3. In what ways is the Solar System a true "system"?
4. What relationship do all of the planets have to the Sun? To each other?

Thinking about the Earth System

5. How does understanding the Earth System help you understand the Solar System?

Thinking about Scientific Inquiry

6. In which parts of the investigation did you:
   a) Make a model?
   b) Use mathematics to solve a problem?
   c) Revise your ideas?
   d) Use your imagination?
   e) Share ideas with others?
   f) Find information from different sources?

Investigation 5:

The Sun and Its Central Role in Our Solar System

Key Question

Before you begin, first think about this key question.

What are the characteristics of the Sun and why is it so important to the Solar System?

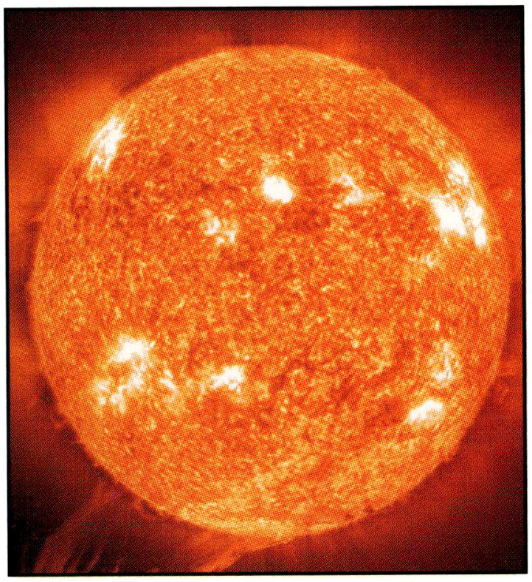

Think about what you know about the Sun. What is the Sun made of? Why is the Sun important to you?

Share your thinking with others in your group and with your class.

In this **Investigation,** you will become more familiar with three important facts about the Sun.

Investigate

Part A: What do you already know about the Sun?

1. You experience the Sun's energy every day. Take a minute and list in your journal all the ways you can think of that the Sun affects your life. (You might want to illustrate your list with pictures.) These sentence stems can help you in your thinking:

   a) The Sun is important because _______.

   b) If we didn't have the Sun, _____.

2. Exchange your ideas about the Sun with other members of your group. Think about these questions:
   - What do we get from the Sun?
   - What place does the Sun have in our Solar System?
   - Where is the Sun in our galaxy?
   - What would we lose if we didn't have the Sun?
   - What reasons can you think of for some ancient peoples worshipping the Sun? Why was it so important to them? (Use your imagination with this question – why would the Sun be so important to early humans who knew very little about science?)
3. Make a three-column table in your journal to organize your thinking about the Sun.
   a) Write your answers to the questions in the table.

Revisit this table when you finish the Solar Lab and have read the **Digging Deeper** section. The Solar Lab will help you to understand more about the Sun, how it works, and why it is important in the Solar System. The Solar Lab is set up in stations, so that you and members of your group can work together to explore the Sun's energy and how it produces that energy.

Inquiry

Charts and Tables

Charts and tables organize a lot of information in a small amount of space. They can be useful because they allow you to focus on important points. In this investigation you will be using a table to organize what you know about the Sun and compare it to what scientists know.

Thinking about the Sun

Sun Questions	My Answers	Scientists' Answers
What do we get from the Sun?		
What place does the Sun have in our Solar System?		
Where is the Sun in our galaxy?		
What would we lose if we didn't have the Sun?		
What reasons can you think of for some ancient peoples worshipping the Sun? Why was it so important to them?		
Other questions about the Sun.		

Part B: Solar Lab

Solar Lab Station 1: The Electromagnetic Spectrum

You have probably already learned a little about light in other science courses. Visible light is part of the electromagnetic (EM) spectrum – the energy we receive from our star, the Sun.

You can see from the diagram that the longer wavelengths are on the left side of the spectrum and that the wavelengths get shorter as you travel to the right side. You feel infrared radiation as heat. You may also be familiar with black light, which is actually ultraviolet radiation.

1. Shine the flashlight through the prism onto a dark surface and see for yourself what colors are in the visible light spectrum.
   a) Use colored pencils to draw in your journal what you see.
2. Use your drawing and the explanation above to answer the following questions:
   a) Which color of light seems to be bent the *most* by the prism?
   b) Which color of light seems to be bent the *least*?

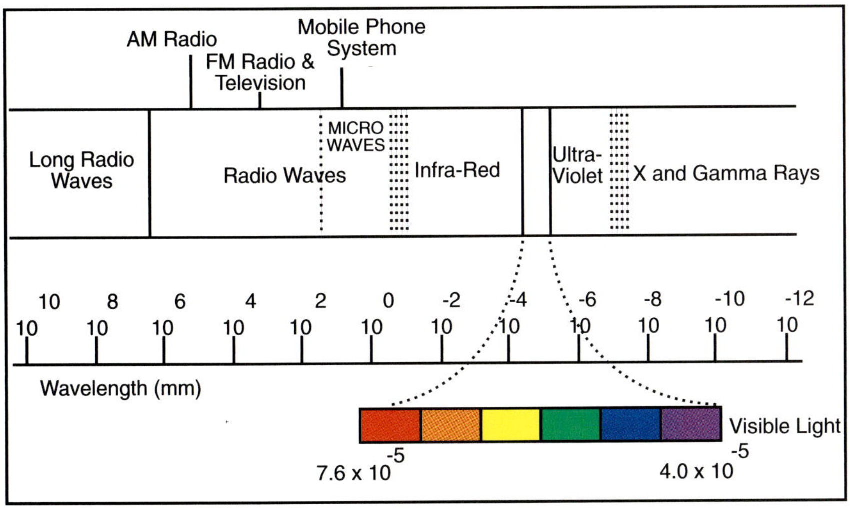

The electromagnetic spectrum shows how different wavelengths represent different types of energy.

Materials Needed

For Station 1, your group will need:

- triangular prism
- flashlight with a strong narrow beam
- colored pencils

c) Of the colors in the visible light spectrum you can see, which has the longest wavelength?

3. Look again at the diagram of the EM spectrum.

   a) In your journal, make a list of ways that you think life on Earth would change if we didn't have this energy from the Sun.

Materials Needed

For Station 2, your group will need:

- plant that has been kept in a closet for a week
- plant that has been kept in the sunlight

Solar Lab Station 2: Plants and the Sun's Energy

At this station, you will see two plants that have the same type of soil and were watered the same amount every day.

1. Observe the two plants. One plant has been exposed to sunlight on a day to day basis, and the other plant has been kept in a closet for a week.

   a) What differences do you observe between the two plants? How might you explain this?

   b) What do you think would happen to the plant kept in the closet if it were never put in the Sun again? Why do you think that is so?

   c) What do you think the relationship is between the Sun and plants on Earth?

   d) How much do animals on the Earth depend on plants? What might happen to animal life on the planet without the Sun's energy?

2. As a group, design an experiment that you could do that would further test these ideas. Can you think of a way to test the impact of the sunlight on only the plant leaves?

   a) Write down your steps, the materials you would need, and your procedure for your teacher to review.

   b) Even if you do not conduct the experiment, what do you think you would be able to learn from this experience?

Solar Lab Station 3: Heat from the Sun

1. At this station, you will have the opportunity to investigate the Sun's infrared (heat) energy.
   a) Draw a table in your journal like the one below.

Temperature Readings (degrees Celsius)			
	0 minutes	5 minutes	10 minutes
Thermometer under paper			
Thermometer in direct sunlight			

2. There are two thermometers under a sheet of paper at this station.
   a) Lift the paper and record the temperatures of both thermometers.
   b) Place one thermometer back under the paper and put the second thermometer into direct sunlight. Wait five minutes, and then record the temperatures again.

Materials Needed

For Station 3, your group will need:

- two thermometers
- sheet of paper

Inquiry

Quantitative and Qualitative Observations

Observations dealing with numbers are called quantitative observations. An example of a quantitative observation is temperature recorded in degrees Celsius. Qualitative observations refer to the qualities of the object. Color is often recorded qualitatively as yellow or green, for example. Some observations can be made either qualitatively or quantitatively, depending on what tools are available and the level of accuracy needed. In this investigation you are making both qualitative and quantitative observations.

c) Wait an additional five minutes, and then record the final temperatures.

3. Write the answers to the following questions in your journal:

   a) What can you conclude about the effect of the direct sunlight on the thermometer?

   b) Did the energy of the Sun have any effect at all on the thermometer under the paper? Why do you think that?

Materials Needed

For this part of the investigation your group will need:

- poster board and colored pencils

Part C: Sharing and Discussing Your Findings

1. When you finish all the stations in the Solar Lab, return to your table of questions about the Sun, from the beginning of this investigation.

   a) Change any answers that were incorrect or incomplete.

   b) Work with your group to come up with as complete a picture of the role of the Sun in the Solar System as possible.

2. As a group, create an informative, yet interesting and colorful, poster about the Sun. The poster should focus on how the Sun and the energy from the Sun has an impact on life on Earth as well as general facts about the Sun.

3. Share your posters with the other students in your class.

Digging Deeper

OUR SUN: A FAMILIAR OBJECT

The Sun is the probably the most prominent object in the sky because of its great size and the enormous amount of energy it releases. The Sun contains 99% of all the matter within the Solar System. It has 300,000 times more mass than the Earth and more than 1,295,000 times more volume. During the day, you can watch what appears to be the Sun's journey across the sky as the Earth receives the Sun's energy. This energy is a strong driving force in the Earth system. It heats the surface of the Earth and makes life possible. At night, the Sun's rays illuminate the Moon. Without the Sun, the Earth would be a dark frozen mass drifting through space.

The Reason For the Seasons

The tilt of the Earth's axis changes over the course of about 41,000 years between an angle of 22° and an angle of 25° as the Earth revolves around the Sun. For part of

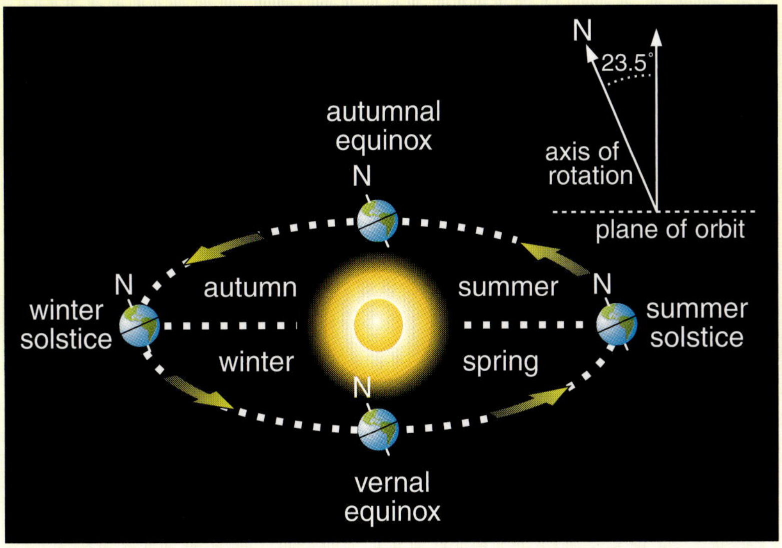

The tilt of the Earth on its axis and its rotation around the Sun cause the seasons.

As You Read...
Think about:

1. ***How is the tilt of the Earth's axis related to the seasons?***
2. ***What is the result of the spreading effect of the solar energy over the surface of the Earth?***
3. ***Why is noon usually the hottest part of the day?***
4. ***Why is the Sun important to our Solar System?***
5. ***Where is our Sun in the universe?***
6. ***What are some of the Sun's special features?***

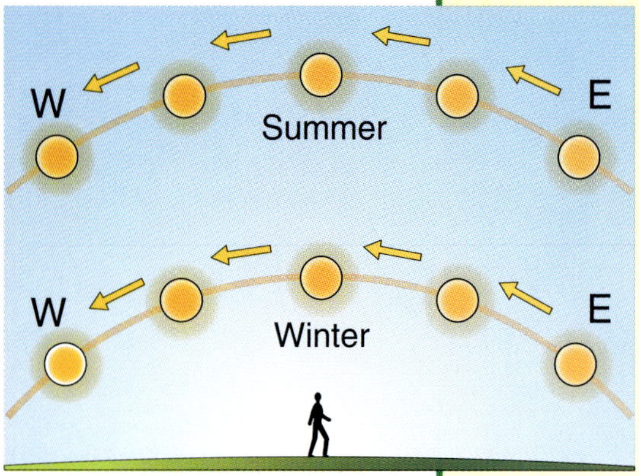

In the summer, the Sun is higher in the sky than in the winter.

the year (summer), the Northern Hemisphere tips towards the Sun. During that same time, the Southern Hemisphere is having winter, since it is tipped away from the Sun.

When either of the Northern or Southern Hemispheres is tipped towards the Sun, two things happen. First, the Sun is visible for more hours of the day, providing more heat energy. Second, the Sun is higher in the sky at noon and shines more directly on the Earth's surface than any other time.

Six months later, the Earth is halfway through its orbit and the same hemisphere is tilted away from the Sun. During this time, the Sun is lower in the sky and the days are shorter. Also, the Sun's energy is spread over the Earth's surface. These effects result in the cooler temperatures of winter. Each year, the cycle of the seasons repeats itself because of the regular and predictable orbit of the Earth around the Sun.

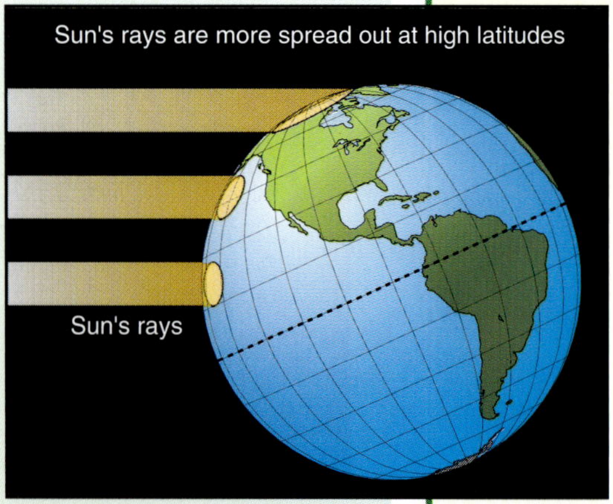

The Earth's tilt and curved surface cause the Sun's rays to be more spread out at high latitudes.

The Earth's curved surface affects how much of the Sun's (solar) energy the Earth receives. A greater angle between the Sun's rays and the Earth's surface causes energy to be spread over a larger area. When is the hottest part of day? It is usually around noon when the Sun is high in the sky and its energy is concentrated on the surface of the Earth.

The spreading effect of solar energy on the Earth's surface creates different temperatures at different points on the Earth. The direct concentration of solar energy on the Earth's Equator causes it to be much warmer than the poles. The spreading effect also causes the Northern and Southern Hemispheres to experience opposite seasons throughout the year.

What is the Sun?

The Sun, the center of our Solar System, is an enormous ball of glowing gas. Most of the Sun is made of hydrogen, one of the simplest atoms in nature. It has a nucleus with one proton at its center and one electron orbiting around it. In the core of the Sun, these protons combine to create new nuclei of helium. This reaction is known as hydrogen fusion. It produces huge amounts of energy that cause the Sun to glow.

The reactions within the Sun produce a huge amount of energy that cause the Sun to glow.

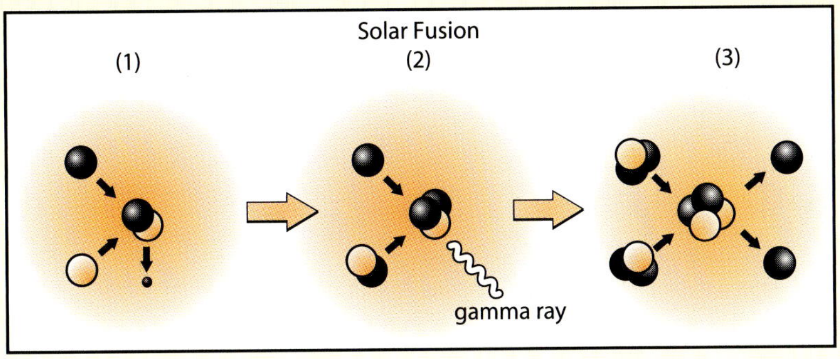

(1) Nuclei of two hydrogen atoms collide in a high-temperature environment. Particles and energy are released. A two-part atom is formed.
(2) Hydrogen nuclei collide with the two-part atom. A three-part helium atom is formed. More energy is released as well as gamma rays.
(3) Two three-part helium atoms collide to form a four-part helium atom. More energy is released as well as a pair of hydrogen atoms.

Structure of the Sun

Like the Earth, the Sun has a layered structure. The outer part of the Sun consists of an atmosphere known as the corona. This layer extends millions of kilometers into space. Temperatures in the corona can get as high as 1,000,000°C. Its gases are so hot that the Sun's gravity

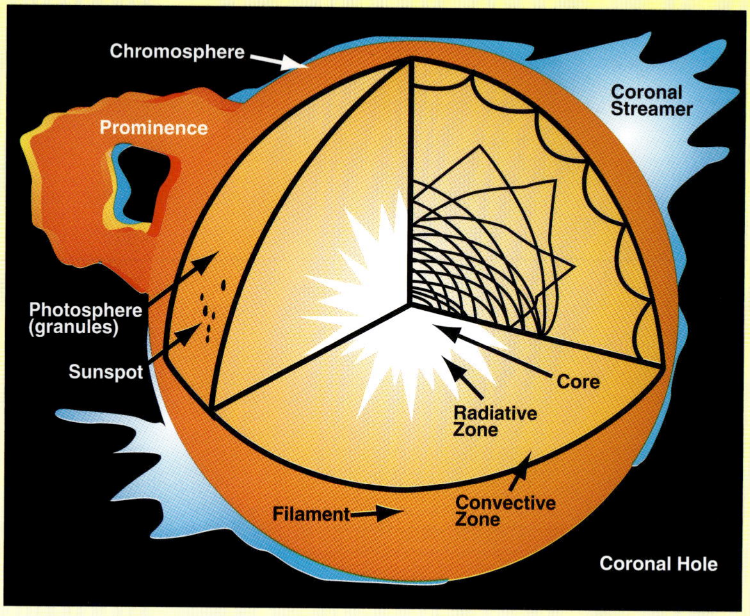

Temperatures vary in the Sun's different layers.

cannot hold them and they escape into space. Below the corona is the irregular surface of the Sun, called the photosphere. This is the visible surface of the Sun and the layer that produces light. Between these two layers is the chromosphere. The temperatures in this layer range from 6000°C to 20,000°C. This layer has a reddish appearance and extends about 2500 km above the photosphere.

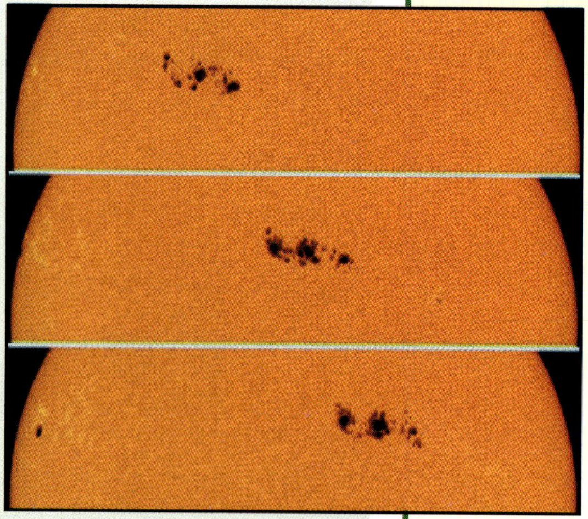

The dark irregular shapes on the surface of the Sun are sunspots.

Surface Features of the Sun

From the Earth, the Sun appears to have a smooth surface. This surface is actually not so smooth and contains a number of interesting features.

Sunspots are areas that have an irregular shape and are darker than other parts of the Sun. Sunspots are relatively cooler than the surrounding parts of the Sun, although they are still very hot. They develop in pairs and appear to travel across the surface of the Sun.

Their movement is actually due to the Sun spinning on its axis. Because the Sun is made up of gas, it rotates more quickly at the Equator (about 25 days) than at the poles (about 33 days). Sunspots at the poles take longer to travel around the Sun than at the Equator. The number of sunspots on the Sun increases and decreases during cycles that last about 22 years.

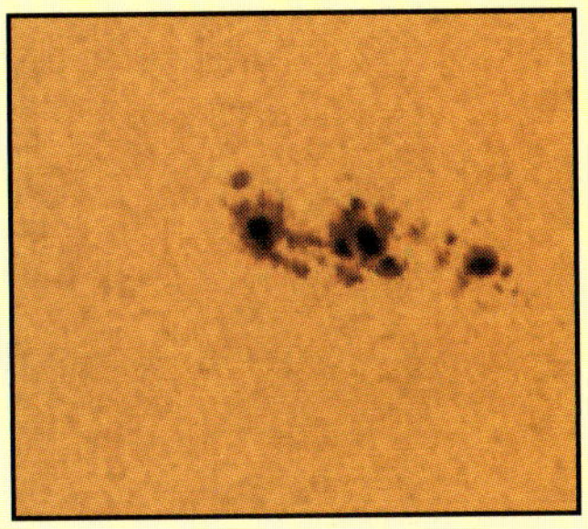

A close-up of a sunspot.

Solar flares are giant explosions of gas on the surface of the Sun. They occur near sunspots and erupt outwards with brilliant colors. During a solar flare, material is heated to millions of degrees Celsius in a matter of minutes. Then it is blasted off the surface. Many forms of energy are released during a solar flare. These include gamma rays and x-rays. Some of the most violent flares can produce enough radiation to be harmful to astronauts or damaging to satellites. Another

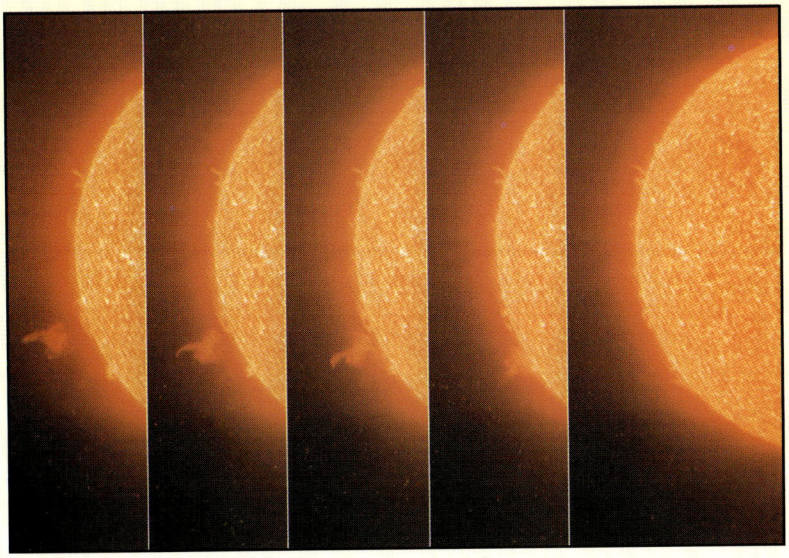

Prominences are huge arcing columns of gas that come from the Sun.

feature of the Sun's surface are huge rising columns of flaming gas called prominences. They are not quite as violent as solar flares and look like feathery red arches.

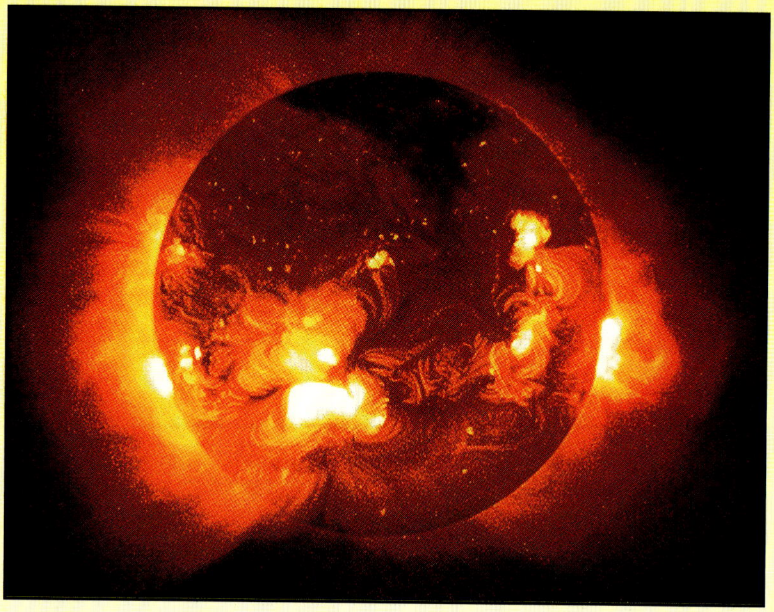

Hot gases in the corona of the Sun cause CMEs to occur.

Coronal mass ejections (CMEs) occur when gases in the corona are so hot that the Sun's gravity cannot hold them. The gases break free from the Sun and form a solar wind. In a single second, this wind can travel 400 km! CMEs take several hours to develop and create one of the largest features in the Sun's atmosphere. Each day, two or three CMEs can occur close to sunspot activity. The solar winds carry magnetic clouds with them. Some of the high-energy particles from these clouds reach the Earth. They can cause problems with communications equipment, including satellites.

Review and Reflect

Review

1. How does the tilt of the Earth produce the seasons?
2. Are the Sun's rays striking the Northern Hemisphere or the Southern Hemisphere more directly when it is summer in North America?
3. When is the hottest part of the day usually? Why?
4. What types of energy does the Sun produce?
5. What evidence do you have that plants need light?
6. What is the role of the Sun in our Solar System?

Reflect

7. How are you personally affected by the change in seasons?
8. Who would be affected more by the change in seasons, someone living close to the Equator or someone living in the far north? Explain.
9. How do humans use the different types of energy in the electromagnetic spectrum?
10. Do you think there would be life on Earth without the Sun? Why do you think that?

What effects does the Sun have on each of the Earth's systems?

11. The Sun is vital to the Earth System. How does the effect of the Sun on one Earth System affect the other systems?

Thinking about Scientific Inquiry

12. In which parts of the investigation did you:
    a) Read for understanding?
    b) Record your own ideas?
    c) Use tools to make measurements?
    d) Make inferences from data?
    e) Share ideas with others?
    f) Find information from different sources?

Investigation 6:

The Planetary Council

Key Question:

Before you begin, first think about this key question.

How are the planets in our Solar System the same and how are they different?

Think about what you have learned so far about the planets in the Solar System. What are the names of the planets? Are they different sizes? Which ones are large and which ones are small?

Share your thinking with others in your group and in the class.

Investigate

In **Investigation 4**, you started to think about the planets in our Solar System. You studied their location in relation to one another and their different sizes. In this investigation, you will learn how the planets are alike and how they are different.

1. In this investigation, you will be role-playing researchers in a space program. Each group in your class will represent a different planet in our Solar System (excluding the Earth). There is only a limited amount of funding to explore the different planets. Each group wants as much research funding as possible for exploring "its planet." For this to happen, you will need to prove to the Planetary Council that your planet should be studied in depth. You will need to make a professional presentation that covers the following points:
   - the features of your planet (size, atmosphere, number of moons, rings, etc.)
   - what evidence there is for how your planet formed

Materials Needed

For this investigation, your group will need:

- resource materials on the planets
- access to the Internet (optional)
- presentation materials (overheads and markers, PowerPoint™ software, computer, computer projector, poster board and markers, photographs, VCR and monitor)

- where the planet is in the Solar System in relation to the Sun and the other planets
- what your planet looks like (use photographs, drawings, video, etc.)
- what interesting questions your research team wants to find out about your planet
- what other objects in, or passing through, the Solar System might have an effect on your planet
- what technology you think could be used to study and/or explore your planet.

2. Once groups have chosen their planets, you will need to decide on research assignments for each group member. Your teacher will have a list of web sites for you to use, and you can also use your school's media center and classroom resources.
3. Plan your presentation. Remember that you want to make the strongest case possible for your planet. You might want to use a PowerPoint™ program to present your information. You might also want to use posters, photos, videos, or overheads. As you research your planet, find out what questions scientists have been asking about it over the years. You will also need to know the latest discoveries that scientists have made about your planet.
4. When you finish your research, outline the important points you need to make in your presentation. Divide up the work fairly, put your presentation together, and rehearse it.
5. Your teacher will arrange a time for the presentations to the Planetary Council. You will need to do a convincing job, so look and act like professional scientists. Be sure to take notes on what the other groups present. That way you can identify what features are the same from planet to planet and what features are different.
6. After each presentation, answer the following questions in your journal:
   a) What is the size of the planet?
   b) How far is it from the Sun?
   c) What is its atmosphere like?
   d) How many moons does the planet have?
   e) What are the unique features of the planet?
   f) What does the planet look like?
   g) What kind of geologic action (if any) occurs on the planet?
7. When all groups have presented, the Planetary Council will decide which groups will receive the major funding.

Inquiry

Ways of Packaging Information

Scientists are often asked to provide information to the public or to make presentations. In doing so, they need to consider both the information they want to communicate and the person or groups that will be using the information. Then they must decide on the best method of packaging and delivering that information. These are decisions you need to make in this investigation.

As You Read...
Think about:

1. ***What is the difference between meteors, meteoroids, and meteorites?***
2. ***What happens when a meteor strikes the Earth?***
3. ***What are asteroids? Can an asteroid strike the Earth?***
4. ***What are comets?***
5. ***What is the relationship between a nebula and the objects in our Solar System?***

Digging Deeper

METEOROIDS

A shooting star streaking through the night sky

Have you ever looked into the night sky and seen the bright streak of a shooting star? If you have, what you have really observed is a small meteoroid entering the Earth's atmosphere.

Meteoroids are small, rocky bodies that revolve around the Sun. If the Earth's orbit crosses the orbit of a meteoroid, the meteoroid may enter into the Earth's atmosphere. When this happens, the meteoroid starts to burn up and creates a streak of light. During its journey through Earth's atmosphere, the meteoroid is known as a meteor. If the meteoroid does not completely burn up and hits the Earth's ground, it is called a meteorite. Each year, the Earth gains about ninety million kilograms of matter from meteorites. Most are small specks, but some are quite large. The largest meteorite ever found was in Africa and weighed more than 54,000 kg!

Meteoroids enter the atmosphere at speeds of several thousand meters per second. The friction of the atmosphere slows down most meteoroids. Only meteoroids larger than a few hundred tons make craters when they strike the Earth. One example of a meteorite crater is in Arizona. This crater formed about 50,000 years ago and is 1200 m in diameter and 50 m deep.

ASTEROIDS

The Barringer meteorite impact crater in Arizona.

Asteroids are bodies of metallic and rocky material, sometimes called minor planets. They orbit the Sun like meteoroids, but are much larger in size. Most asteroids are located in a wide region of the Solar System called the Main Asteroid Belt. This belt of asteroids is like a giant doughnut-shaped ring between the orbits of Mars and Jupiter. During the early development of the Solar System, the strong gravity of Jupiter kept the asteroids in the Main Asteroid Belt from forming into a planet.

Asteroids that come close to our planet are known as near-Earth asteroids. The largest near-Earth asteroid is called 1036 Ganymede, and is 41 km in diameter. Scientists think that near-Earth asteroids are produced by the collision of asteroids within the Main Asteroid Belt. At least a thousand asteroids larger than 1 km in diameter have orbits that cross the orbit of the Earth. Sometimes these near-Earth asteroids collide with the Earth. About 65 million years ago, an asteroid 10 km across struck the Earth. The after-effects of this collision may have been responsible for the extinction of the dinosaurs.

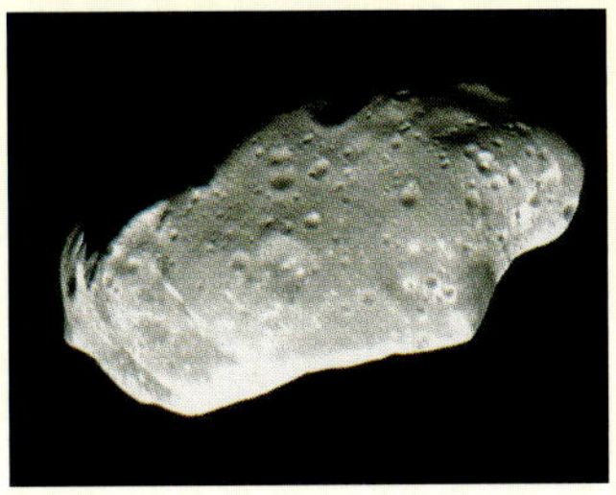

A close-up of an asteroid.

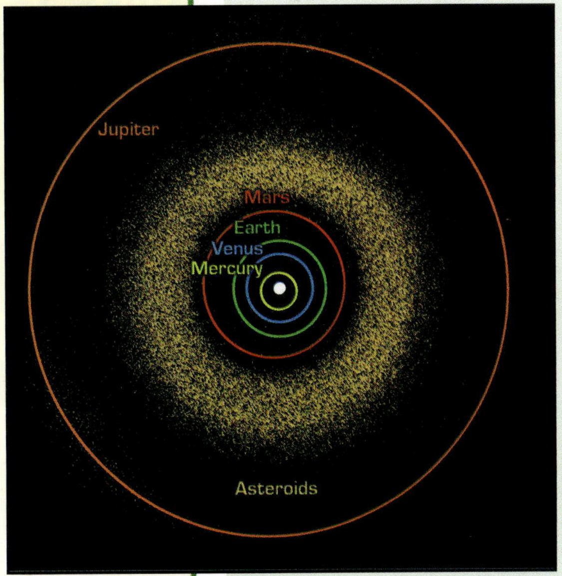

The Main Asteroid Belt is located between Mars and Jupiter.

Ice turns into a gas to form the streaming tail of a comet.

COMETS

Most comets can only be seen with a telescope but some pass close enough to Earth to be observed with the naked eye. A very bright comet can be seen in the night sky for days, weeks, or even months. A comet is a small body of ice, rock and dust that is loosely packed together. It can be thought of as an enormous snowball made of frozen gases that contains very little solid material. Comets, like planets, also orbit the Sun.

When a comet comes close enough to the Sun, the solar energy turns some of the ice into a gas. This vapor can be seen streaming behind the comet like a tail. Although very low in mass, comets are one of the largest members of the Solar System. The frozen part of a comet is only a few tens of kilometers at most. A comet's head can be as large as 100,000 km across. Its tail can be tens of millions of kilometers long.

One of the most famous of Earth's visiting comets is called Halley's comet, which was last seen in 1986. It passes by Earth every 76 years and will next appear in 2062.

NEBULAR THEORY

Most scientists agree that the objects in the Solar System formed about 4.6 billion years ago from a giant cloud of swirling gas and dust. This cloud is called a nebula, and its matter was probably thrown off from other stars in our region of the galaxy. Gravity caused the gases and dust to be drawn together, making the giant cloud fall inwards. As it collapsed, it got flatter,

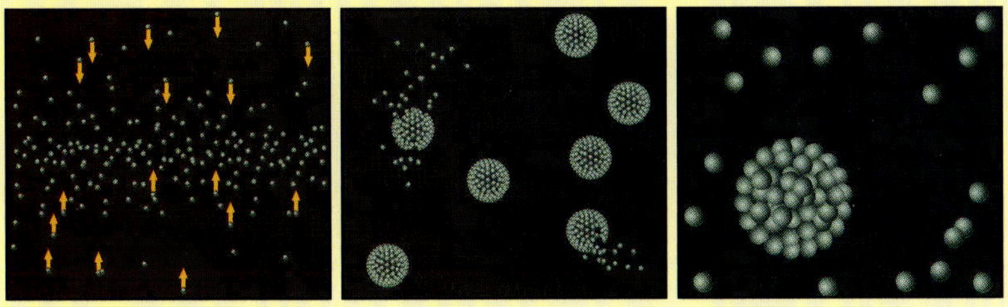

Particles within the nebula cloud were pulled together by gravity.

began to rotate and took the shape of a disk. The collapsing matter in the center of the disk eventually formed the Sun.

In the hot, inner part of the young Solar System, rock and metals with high freezing-point temperature remained solid. Here, the terrestrial planets formed as dense rocky worlds. The terrestrial planets include Mercury, Venus, Earth, and Mars. Farther from the Sun, the temperatures were lower. At this point, gas and icy particles (bits of matter) formed different types of planets. As the mass and gravity of these planets increased, they started to attract more particles. They

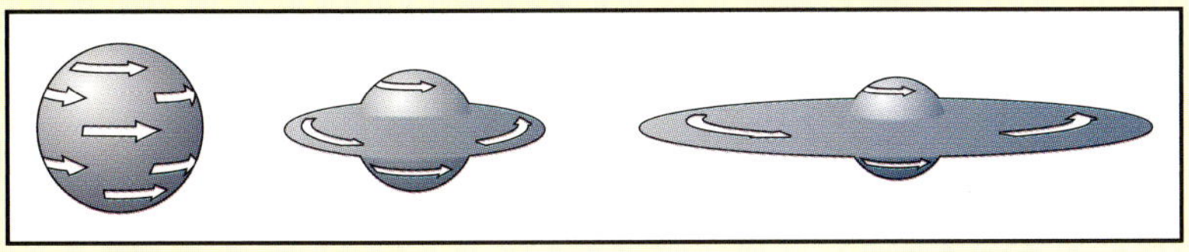

The Sun formed from a giant cloud of swirling gas and dust.

grew into the gigantic outer planets we call the gas giants. The gas giants include Jupiter, Saturn, Uranus, and Neptune.

Powerful telescopes have provided scientists with images of other stars and planets forming in the depths of giant clouds and rotating disks of gas and dust. Scientists have used the images as evidence of nebular theory.

Chandra is an x-ray telescope sent into orbit around the Earth in 1999.

Review and Reflect

Review

1. What did you learn about your planet that you did not know before?
2. What important and interesting questions have scientists asked about your planet?

Reflect

3. What explanation do you have for the similarities between the planets?
4. How are the planets different? Make a list of those differences as well.
5. How can you explain the differences between the planets?

Thinking about the Earth System

6. How are meteoroids and asteroids connected to the Earth System?
7. How does the Nebular Theory help you understand the structure of the Earth?

Thinking about Scientific Inquiry

8. In which parts of the investigation did you:
    a) Ask your own questions?
    b) Record your own ideas?
    c) Revise your ideas?
    d) Use your imagination?
    e) Share ideas with others?
    f) Find information from different sources?
    g) Pull your information together to make a presentation?

Investigation 7:

What is Beyond Our Solar System?

Key Question

Before you begin, first think about this key question.

What are the other major objects in our universe and what are they like?

Think about what you have learned about the Solar System. What is beyond our Solar System?

Share your thinking with others in your group and in your class.

You have spent quite a bit of time in this module studying the objects in our own Solar System. You should now know about the role of the Sun, the names and characteristics of the planets (including the Earth), and the structure of the Solar System. You should also know the role of gravity in orbital paths, and how our Moon is related to and affects the Earth. In this investigation, you will move beyond our Solar System to learn about stars, galaxies, nebulae, and theories of how the universe was formed.

Investigate

Human beings have always been fascinated by stars and constellations. Constellations are the patterns stars make in the night sky. Knowing about the constellations and where they appear in the sky at different times of the year is useful in identifying individual stars.

Materials Needed

For this investigation, your group will need:

- star chart
- glow-in-the-dark stars
- large sheet of black construction paper
- small flashlight with a very powerful beam
- large flashlight with a dim beam
- metric measuring tape
- CD-ROM on the universe (optional)

Part A: How Stars Look to Our Eyes

1. To get a sense of the relationship between the brightness of stars and their distance from Earth, your group will try a little demonstration. You will need a strong flashlight and a much weaker flashlight to do this.
2. Two members of your group will each take a flashlight. The other members will stand at a distance of at least 10 m away.
3. The students with the flashlights will turn on both flashlights, in a large darkened area. The observers will note the differences in the way that the flashlights appear.
4. As a group, brainstorm how the flashlights could be arranged so that they appear to be the same brightness to the observers. Try different ideas until the flashlights appear to be the same brightness to the observers.
   a) Record the steps you took and the end locations of each flashlight in your journals.
5. Answer the following questions in your journal:
   a) What did you have to do to make both lights look about the same?
   b) What might that tell you about the stars that you see in the night sky?
   c) Do you think all stars are the same distance from the Earth? What evidence do you have for or against this idea?
   d) If your class has access to computers with an Internet link-up, see what you can find out about stars and their distance from the Earth on the NASA web site: www.nasa.gov. Did this information match your group's ideas about stars and how they appear from the Earth?
   e) What else can you find from the NASA site about how stars appear to twinkle from the Earth? Find this out and share it with other groups in your class.

Inquiry

Initial Experiments

Often, a scientific investigation begins with a simple informal experiment to test a prediction. The results may not solve the problem, but they may be useful in later investigations. In this part of the investigation, you did a simple demonstration to start you thinking about whether all the stars you see at night are the same distance from the Earth.

Part B: Your "Specialist" Constellation

1. Your teacher will give you a "map" of the night sky at a particular time of the year. Work with your group to decide on a constellation that you find really interesting. You may have heard about one in language arts studying mythologies of different cultures.
2. Once your group has agreed upon its constellation, find out the following information about it to share with other groups in your class.
   a) How did it get its name and is there any story behind that?
   b) What stars are in it?
   c) How does it appear to change its position with the seasons?
   d) What "famous" stars are in it?
3. Use glow-in the-dark stars to "make" your constellation on a sheet of black construction paper. You will also need to become aware of where this constellation is in relation to other constellations in the sky. Your teacher will later hang the constellation posters on the ceiling in their proper locations.
4. Once all the constellations are on the ceiling, turn off the classroom lights. Have a whole group session during which each group explains the facts about its constellation to the other groups.
   a) Make notes on the other constellations so that you can ask questions about them later on.

Inquiry

Using References

When you write a science report, the information you gather from books, magazines, and the Internet comes from evidence gathered by others. You must always list the source of your evidence. This not only gives credit to the person who wrote the work, but it allows others to examine it and decide for themselves whether or not it makes sense.

Part C: Galaxies, Nebulae, and the Origin of the Universe

1. Examine the photographs of galaxies taken by one of the Great Observatories.

   a) Examine the pictures closely. What other galaxies do you see? How do the galaxies seem to be similar? How are they different?

   b) In your journal, make a table like the one below. As you study your galaxy photographs, fill in the table as best you can. You will also want to refer to the **Digging Deeper** on Galaxies and Nebulae to help you out.

Name of the Galaxy	Shape of the Galaxy	Important Stars in the Galaxy	Other Interesting Facts About the Galaxy

2. Now, examine the pictures that you have of nebulae (the plural of nebula) in the same way. You already know that nebulae are enormous clouds of dust and gas in the universe.

   a) How are the nebulae the same and how they are different?

   b) In your journal, make a table like the one below for nebulae. Complete the information, again, using the information on Galaxies and Nebulae for help.

Name of the Nebula	Shape of the Nebula	Type of Nebula	Other Interesting Facts About the Nebula

3. When you finish, compare what you have discovered about galaxies and nebulae with another group.
   a) Share your information and make your tables as complete and accurate as you can. Keep these tables handy for the **Review and Reflect** questions at the end of this investigation.

Part D: Theories About How the Universe Began

Over the years, scientists have had many theories about how the universe began. It has always been very difficult, however, to collect evidence that would support these theories. With advancing technologies, though, scientists have been able to collect data that seem to support one or two major theories. In this last part of the investigation, you will search the **Digging Deeper** section for evidence supporting one of these, the "Big Bang" Theory.

1. You will first need to find out what the Big Bang Theory is.
   a) What does it seem to explain about the universe and who came up with it in the first place?
2. Use the evidence about the Big Bang Theory in the **Digging Deeper** section.
   a) Work with your group to write an argument supporting the Big Bang Theory.
3. When you finish, share your argument with the class. Listen to what other groups say about the theory. They may have spotted evidence that your group missed.
   a) How complete, do you think, is the evidence of the Big Bang Theory?
   b) What appears to be missing in the evidence?
   c) How much sense does the evidence make to you? How useful is the theory in thinking about the universe?

Inquiry

Using References as Evidence

When you write a science report, the information you gather from books, magazines, and the Internet comes from science investigations. Just as in your experiments, the results can be used as evidence. Sometimes, enough new evidence accumulates that make ideas change drastically. This is true of the theories about how the universe began.

As You Read...

Think about:

1. ***What are galaxies and how are they classified?***
2. ***Where are we in the Milky Way Galaxy?***
3. ***What do scientists think "black holes" are?***
4. ***What is the "Big Bang Theory"? What is the evidence for this theory?***

M84 (lenticular): Sixty million light-years away.

Virgo A or M87 (giant elliptical): Sixty million light-years away.

Digging Deeper

GALAXIES AND NEBULAE

Galaxies

Galaxies are large systems of stars, nebulae, and the matter between the stars (interstellar matter). A number of galaxies were discovered and cataloged by Charles Messier in the late 1700s. Messier's telescope did not have the resolution necessary to see individual stars in the galaxies and he referred to them as nebula.

Milky Way Galaxy (spiral): This is our own galaxy. It is 100,000 light-years in diameter.

Andromeda Galaxy (spiral): This is a relatively close spiral galaxy similar to our own (2–3 light-years away).

Types of Galaxies

- **Spiral:** These galaxies have a large central disc with clusters of young stars and lots of matter between the stars and a bulge component of older stars.
- **Lenticular:** These galaxies are "smooth disc" galaxies of older stars. They have used up the material between the stars.
- **Elliptical:** These galaxies are football-shaped galaxies of older stars with little or no material between the stars.

- **Irregular:** These galaxies are those that don't fit into the other categories.

Nebula

A nebula is an enormous cloud of gas and/or dust in space. Nebulae are the birthplaces of stars.

Types of Nebulae

- **Emission Nebulae:** These are clouds of gas, which glow by re-emitting the ultra-violet radiation absorbed from young hot stars. These nebulae usually look reddish and are the source of recent star formation.
- **Reflection Nebulae:** These are clouds of dust that reflect the light of nearby stars. They usually look blue and are also the source of star formation.
- **Dark Nebulae:** These are usually about a few hundred light-years in width. Dark nebulae are clouds of dust that block the light from behind them.
- **Planetary Nebulae:** These are relatively small clouds of dust given off by dwarf stars as they near the end of their lives.
- **Supernova Remnants:** These are a relatively small (few light-years across) part of a massive star that is left over after the star ends its life in a supernova explosion.

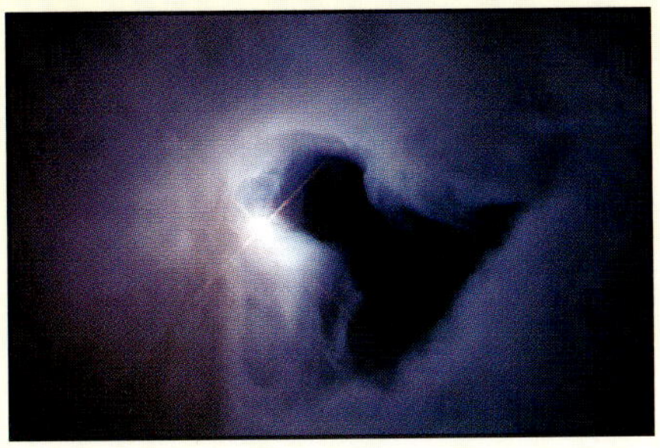

NGC 1999, a nebula in the constellation Oriion. (reflection)

Stars are formed from giant nebula clouds.

Horsehead Nebula (dark nebula at the center).

Orion Nebula (emission).

The Milky Way.

The Milky Way Galaxy

Our Solar System is located in a galaxy known as the Milky Way Galaxy. The Milky Way Galaxy contains more than 100 billion stars, each of which may have orbiting planets and other objects. The Milky Way Galaxy is shaped like a spiral, with arms that extend outwards from a bulge at its center. Each arm is full of dust, stars, and space. Our Solar System is located on the outside of one of these arms.

The arms of the Milky Way Galaxy rotate on an axis that goes through the middle of the galaxy. This means that just as the planets in our Solar System orbit the Sun, our Solar System orbits around the center of the Milky Way. It takes 240 million years for the Sun to orbit the center of the Milky Way Galaxy!

Scientists believe that many galaxies contain gigantic black holes in their centers. These black holes formed when stars collided as matter moved toward the center of the galaxy during its beginnings. The black holes produce "active" galaxies where there is more energy being emitted than would normally be expected.

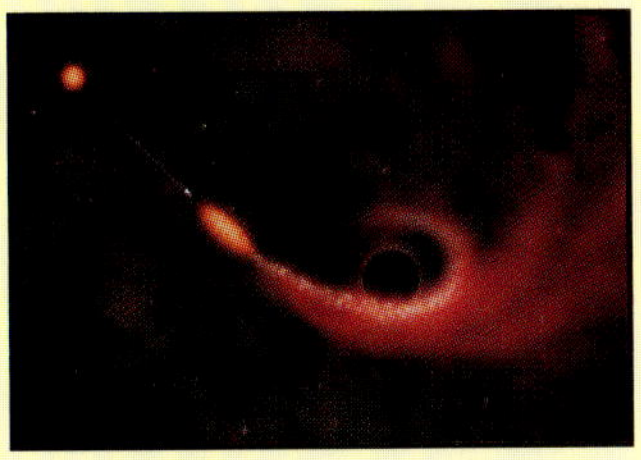

The gravitational pull of a black hole is so intense that nothing can escape, not even light.

In contrast, "normal" galaxies give off energy from their stars without this additional source. Change takes place much more slowly in normal galaxies than in active ones. The Milky Way Galaxy is a normal galaxy.

THE UNIVERSE BEGAN WITH A BANG! (OR DID IT?)

The Big Bang Theory is the most widely accepted explanation among scientists for the origin of the universe. It states that the universe was formed 13.7 billion years ago. In the beginning, everything in the universe was concentrated into a volume that was incredibly small. The matter that made up this tiny universe was very hot and very dense (heavy for its size). The early universe began with space rapidly

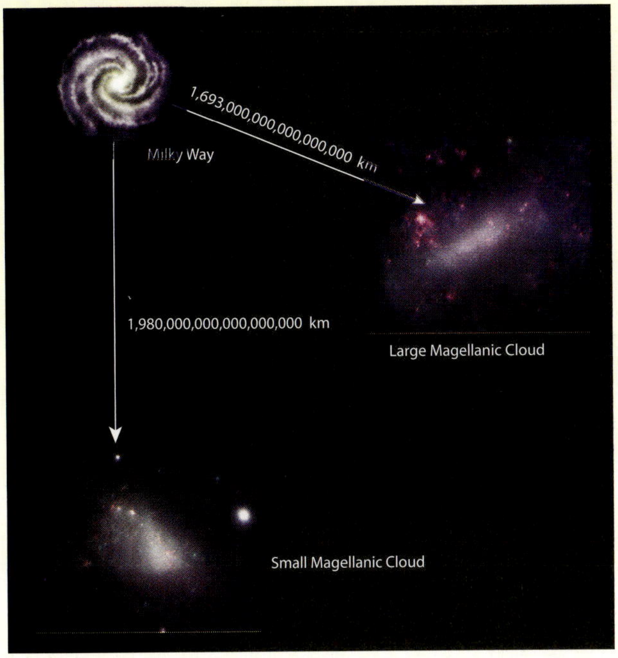

The distances between galaxies are great.

Our Solar System is located in a spiral arm of the Milky Way Galaxy. The stars in the inner bulge of the spiral were the first to form when the Milky Way Galaxy began to develop. Stars in the arms of the spiral formed later and are younger than those in the bulge.

expanding carrying matter along with it. The Big Bang Theory also states that the universe is still expanding. Distant galaxies are traveling away from each other at great speeds.

Evidence of the Big Bang

The Big Bang Theory explains only the expansion of the universe. It does not attempt to explain how this process began. Nor does it explain what is beyond the edge of the universe. As with many strong theories, its strength comes from making a clear statement that is supported by solid evidence.

Stronger telescopes in the 20th century helped many astronomers investigate faraway galaxies and the Big Bang Theory. In 1929, Edward Hubble discovered that the more distant a galaxy is from our galaxy, the faster it is moving away from us. Specialized astronomers who study the origin and expansion of the universe are known as cosmologists.

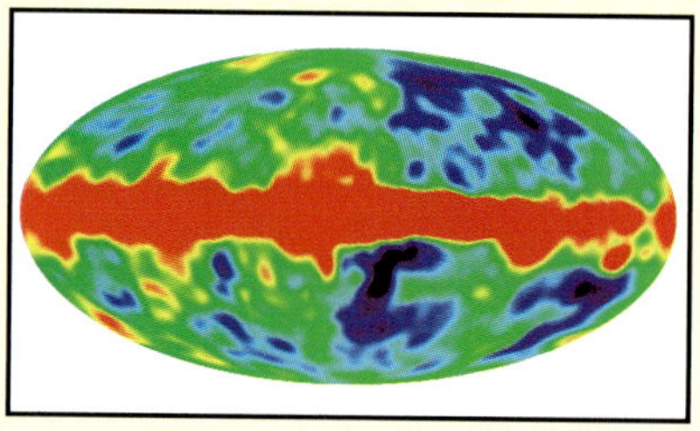

A microwave map of the Universe produced by the Wilkinson probe.

Cosmologists study the universe by using probes that look out into space. These probes detect the energy released during the initial moments of the Big Bang. This energy has been detected by these probes coming in from all directions of the universe.

By studying the light from distant galaxies and the energy from the edges of the universe, scientists are actually looking back through time.

The Wilkinson probe mapping the edge of the universe.

A STAR IS BORN

Astronomers believe that a star begins to form when particles in a dense region of a gas and dust cloud nebula are pulled toward each other. This collapse is caused by gravitation as the particles move inwards toward the center of the nebula to form the star. Eventually, enough particles collect to make the star dense enough to produce energy. Most of the energy produced is by hydrogen nuclei joining together, deep in the star's center to form helium nuclei. This process is called hydrogen fusion.

Main-Sequence Stars

The diagram shows the relationship between a star's brightness and its temperature. The stars in the diagram are categorized into one of three types: white dwarfs, main-sequence stars, and supergiants and giants. The stars in the main-sequence section show that as temperature increases, brightness increases. About 90% of the stars in the universe fit into this sequence. The

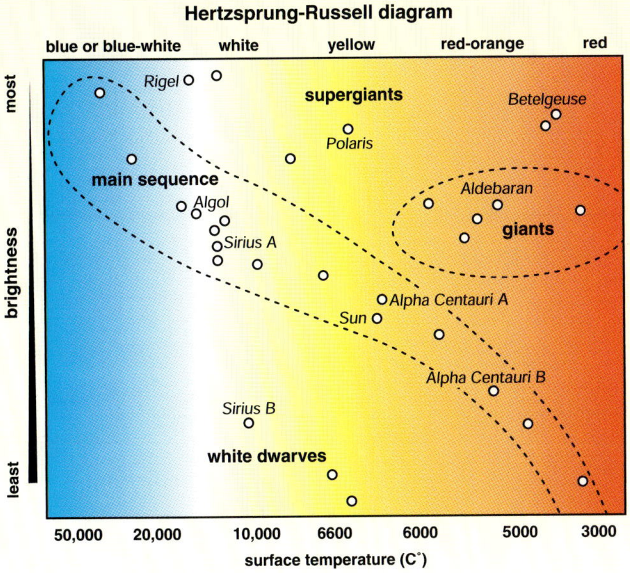

diagram also shows that as stars become cooler, they also become dimmer. As their brightness *decreases*, they change color from bright blue to dim red. The white dwarfs are small stars that are very hot, but not very bright. Supergiants and red giants are brighter than the hottest main-sequence stars. These stars are not as hot as the blue stars in the sequence.

The Life Cycle of a Star

The temperature of stars is so high that they cause nuclei of hydrogen to fuse together to create helium atoms in a process called fusion. For this reaction to occur, four hydrogen nuclei must combine to form a single helium nucleus. During this reaction, a small amount of mass is lost and converted into a massive amount of energy. All stars have a limited supply of hydrogen that can be fused into helium. Once the hydrogen is used up, the star goes through some big changes.

A picture of a giant galactic nebula, showing various stages of the life cycle of stars in one single view.

When main-sequence stars use up their hydrogen atoms, they become giant stars. It can take millions to billions of years for a star to deplete its supply of hydrogen. When a main-sequence star uses up its hydrogen supply, it starts to cool. As it cools, it begins to contract and become smaller. The contraction eventually makes the star heat up again causing the star to expand. During this process, its outer layers become much cooler than when it was a main-sequence star. The star is now like a car that is running out of gas. In its next cycle, it swells in size to become a giant star. Our Sun will

Impressions of supernova explosions in neighboring galaxies.

use up its supply of hydrogen and go through this process in about 5 billion years.

White dwarfs form after the hydrogen in a star's core is used up. The star starts to cool and contract and it loses its outer layers into space. Gravity continues to draw matter toward the core of the star and it becomes a hot, very dense star of low brightness.

Giant stars are more than ten times larger than the Sun and can go through violent explosions. In the super-hot cores of giant stars, some of the matter fuses together. The star expands rapidly to a gigantic size. Supergiants form from giant stars and are much larger than the Sun. Eventually, iron forms in the core and energy production comes to an end. Once their hydrogen supply is depleted, their high core temperatures cause violent reactions to occur. The core collapses violently, sending shock waves through the star. This creates a gigantic explosion called a supernova.

HOW DO SCIENTISTS INVESTIGATE OUTER SPACE?

The 2.5-meter reflecting telescope of the Sloan Digital Sky Survey. The box-like structure protects the separately mounted telescope from being buffeted by the wind.

The invention of the telescope during the time of Galileo was one of the most important events in the history of astronomy. This small instrument completely changed how people thought about the stars, planets, and moons in space. It was an extension of human senses and, for the first time, people could see things never before dreamed of. Since Galileo's time, countless telescopes have been designed, each one providing clearer images of objects in space.

Today's optical telescope magnifies objects in space, such as stars and planets, by concentrating the visible light waves they emit or reflect. These telescopes use lenses or mirrors to gather the light from an object. The light is then focused to create a magnified image of that object. There are optical telescopes that are small enough to be carried in your hand, while others are as big as buildings and weigh 300 tons!

The Zeiss 12-inch refracting telescope

The Earth's atmosphere can get in the way of the visible light gathered by optical telescopes. The gases, clouds, and particles in the atmosphere can make the visible light from stars appear blurry or flicker. To prevent this from happening, scientists put their telescopes on mountaintops, where the air is dryer and thinner. There is also less pollution to distort the visible light coming from space.

The Hubble Space Telescope (HST) orbiting above Earth.

In 1990, scientists put the Hubble Space Telescope into orbit above the Earth's atmosphere. In space, there is little to distort the visible light coming from distant objects. It has produced some of the most detailed and clearest images of space ever seen. Hubble is about the size of a large school bus. It travels at an orbital speed of nearly 8 km/s (kilometers per second), or 97 min per orbit. Hubble is powered by energy from the Sun and in an average orbit, uses about the same amount of energy as twenty-eight 100-W light bulbs.

The Arecibo Observatory located in Puerto Rico.

Other telescopes can collect different types of electromagnetic radiation from objects in space. The largest of these are the radio telescopes. They have huge surfaces to receive long radio wavelengths from space objects. Arecibo is the largest radio telescope in the world with its 300-m wide surface built into a hill! There are also ultraviolet telescopes, infrared telescopes,

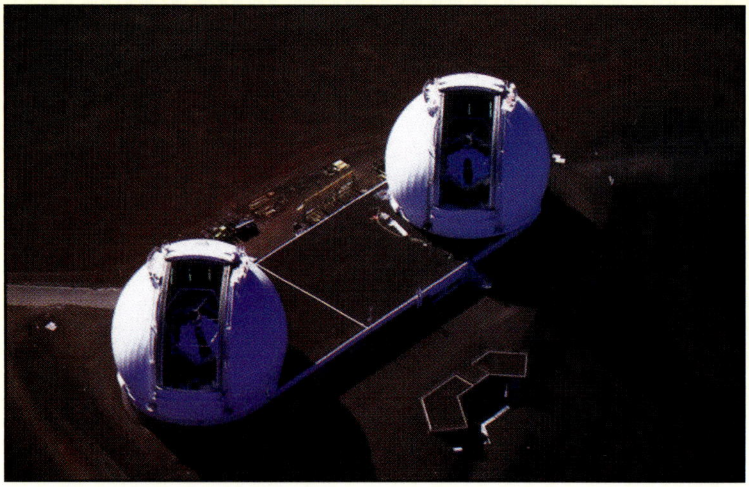

The W. M. Keck Observatory on the summit of Hawaii's dormant Mauna Kea volcano. The twin Keck Telescopes are the world's largest optical and infrared telescopes.

gamma-ray telescopes, and x-ray telescopes. They work in space and collect radiation from above the Earth's atmosphere. Each of these telescopes creates its own image for the data that it is designed to collect.

A human-made object placed in orbit around the Earth is called an artificial satellite. Artificial satellites serve a variety of purposes, including the transmission of signals for television shows and cell phone calls. When a telescope is placed in space above the Earth's atmosphere, it is also an artificial satellite.

Scientists also send research instruments, such as telescopes, that travel into space away from the Earth. These unmanned spacecraft are known as space probes. The first probe was launched in 1959 to collect information about the Earth's Moon. Since that time, dozens of probes have been sent into space to collect information about all the planets of the Solar System, as well as asteroids, comets, and solar wind. Probes have even landed on the surface of Mars!

The first single crewmember EVA capture attempt of the Intelsat VI as seen from Endeavour's aft flight deck windows. EVA Mission Specialist Pierre Thuot standing on the Remote Manipulator System (RMS) end effector platform, with the satellite capture bar attempting to attach it to the free floating communications satellite.

The Mars Pathfinder lands on Mars. The Sojourner used the fully deployed forward ramp at far left, and rear ramp at right, to descend to the surface of Mars on July 5, 1997. Rover tracks lead to Sojourner, shown using its Alpha Proton X-Ray Spectrometer instrument to study the large rock Yogi.

Review and Reflect

Review

1. Explain why you think that stars, although they are incredibly large, can look so tiny to us here on the Earth. Why does our own star, the Sun, look so big?
2. What are constellations? How can you explain how they look different in the sky at various times of the year?
3. What are galaxies? How do scientists classify them?
4. Explain what nebulae are and how they are different from one another.
5. What is the Big Bang Theory? What is one piece of evidence supporting that theory?

Reflect

6. What do you think are the main problems in studying objects in the universe?
7. How has technology helped scientists to learn more about what is in the universe? What new technology do you think would be useful in studying the universe?
8. How well do you think the Big Bang Theory is supported? How confident are you that this theory explains how the universe began?

Thinking about the Earth System

9. What conditions would have to be in place for a planet similar to Earth to exist?

Thinking about Scientific Inquiry

10. In which parts of the investigation did you:
    a) Make models?
    b) Compare ideas?
    c) Revise your ideas?
    d) Use your imagination?
    e) Share ideas with others?
    f) Organize information?
    g) Pull your information together to make a presentation?

Investigation 8:

Discovering the Difference Between Science Fact and Science Fiction

Putting It All Together

Key Question

Before you begin, first think about this key question.

How can you tell the difference between science fact and science fiction?

Think about what you have learned so far about Earth and space. Think about the science fiction movies or television shows you have watched. How are they different?

Share your thinking with others in your class.

There are many ways of communicating information about science. There are scientific journals, conferences, books and web sites. However, these are not the only ways people learn about science. In this investigation, you will first explore ways in which people communicate scientific information. Then you will practice separating science fact from science fiction.

Materials Needed

For this investigation, your group will need:

- communications piece that combines astronomy fact with fiction (teacher's choice)
- materials to develop your own communications piece (video camera, PowerPoint™, computer, poster board, colored pencils)

Investigate

1. With your group, think about and make a list of all the ways you find out about science information every day. Think creatively! There are a lot of choices!

   a) Write your list in your journal.

Which photograph represents science fact and which is science fiction?

2. When you finish with your list, share it with other groups in your class to make a master list.

   a) On the master list, work with your class to make a check mark by any of the items on the list that might have science fact mixed with science fiction.

   b) Be sure to explain why you think that item on the list should be checked. It would help to give a specific example to make your explanation stronger.

3. Your group's task is to create an interesting and creative presentation for the general public on an astronomy topic you have learned about in this module.

   You may present it in any form, such as a comic book, TV show, commercial, movie trailer, but be sure to mix fact and fiction in your piece.

   When you finish, you will present your piece. The job of the other groups in the class will be to figure out which astronomy information is fact and which is fiction.

   You might want to focus on some of the basic science you learned about astronomy, or you might prefer to deal with some of the exciting new findings coming out of the field.

4. To practice how to do this, you will first analyze astronomy fact versus fiction in a movie, story, television show, or some other medium.

   a) As you watch or read the communications piece, make notes on what you think is scientific fact and what appears to be science fiction.

5. When you finish, discuss your notes with your group. Sort the fact from fiction, and then meet with another group to talk over your thoughts. Answer these questions:

a) Why do you think the piece blends fiction with fact?

b) What do the producers of the piece seem to want the readers/viewers to believe?

c) How could you change the piece to make it more factual?

6. Use all of the resources in your classroom, plus your journals, to decide what content will be in your piece.

   Divide up the work so that everyone in your group has a fair share of the effort. Some people might be better at artwork, while others are good writers or researchers.

   a) Outline what you want in your piece, and then do the research you need to make sure that the science content is correct. Be as creative as you can, but don't try to cover a huge topic. Some ideas might be:

   - Water on Mars
   - Remote space travel to distant planets
   - Search for extraterrestrial intelligence
   - U.S. space program compared to other countries' programs
   - Space Shuttle flights
   - New planets
   - The Apollo missions
   - New technologies used for space observation
   - History of astronomy (famous astronomers)
   - Potential space hazards

7. Take your accurate information and decide how you will weave fiction into your piece. It might be useful to limit the fiction to just three or four items, so that your audience isn't overwhelmed.

   a) Create your piece and your presentation. Check with your teacher to make sure that your "accurate" information really is accurate.

8. When everything is ready, your teacher will set up a presentation schedule. You will be responsible both for presenting your piece and analyzing other groups' pieces for fact versus fiction.

Review and Reflect

Review

1. How did other groups capture your interest with science fact?
2. How did they capture your interest with science fiction?

Reflect

3. What use do you think science fiction has in the world?
4. How can you tell science fact from fiction in your everyday life? What would you look for? What resources could you use to help you figure out fact from fiction?

Thinking about Scientific Inquiry

5. In which parts of the investigation did you:
   a) Analyze information?
   b) Compare ideas?
   c) Revise your ideas?
   d) Use your imagination?
   e) Share ideas with others?
   f) Organize information?
   g) Pull your information together to make a presentation?

Reflecting

Back to the Beginning

How have your ideas about the Earth in Space changed from when you started? Look at following items carefully. Draw and write down the ideas you have now about these items. How have your ideas changed?

- Your original sketch of the Solar System with labels.
- Your explanation of what gravity is.
- Your list of all the objects you know about that are outside the Solar System.
- The explanation of two of the items from your list of objects in space and the explanation of what they are.

Thinking about the Earth System

The investigations in this module have had you looking at the Earth, the Solar System, and beyond. Think about the idea of "systems within systems." Answer the following question in your journal:

- What connections can you make between Earth in Space and the Earth System?

Thinking about Scientific Inquiry

Review the investigations you have done and the inquiry processes you have used. Answer the following questions in your journal:

- What scientific processes did you use?
- How did scientific inquiry processes help you learn about Earth in Space?

A New Beginning

This investigation into Earth in Space and astronomy is now complete, but that's not the end of the story! As time goes by, you will see, and hear about, many new space-science events and discoveries. Maybe you will actually travel in space one day. Be alert for opportunities to add to your knowledge and understanding.

The Big Picture

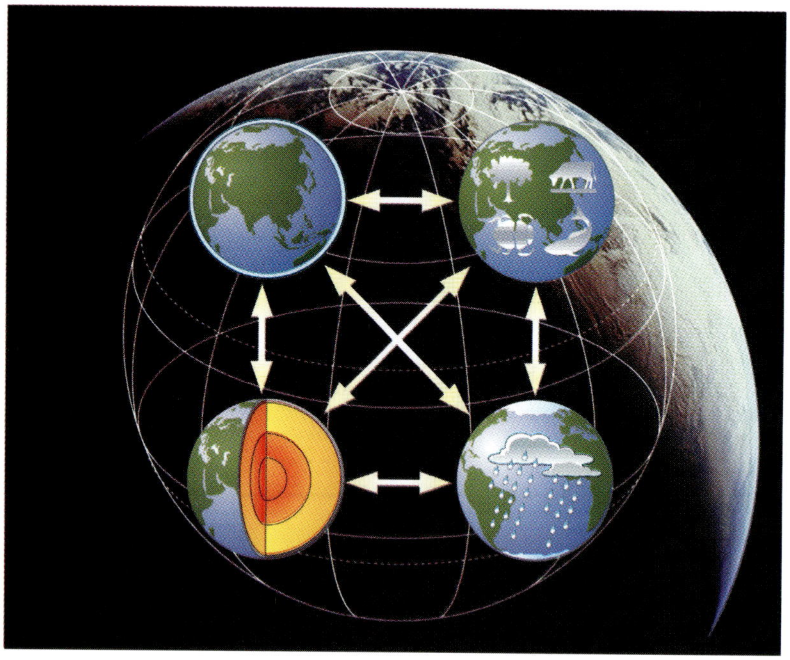

Key Concepts

Earth is a set of closely linked systems.

Earth's processes are powered by two sources: the Sun, and Earth's own inner heat.

The geology of Earth is dynamic, and has evolved over 4.6 billion years.

The geological evolution of Earth has left a record of its history that geoscientists interpret.

We depend upon Earth's resources—both mined and grown.

Glossary

Asteroid – A small planetary body in orbit around the Sun, larger than a meteoroid but smaller than a planet. Many asteroids can be found in a belt between the orbits of Mars and Jupiter.

Astronomical unit – A unit of measure equal to the average distance between the Sun and the Earth, about 149,600,000 km (1.496×10^8 km).

Atmosphere – A thin layer composed of a mixture of gases that surrounds the Earth. Earth's gravity holds the atmosphere in place.

Big Bang Theory – The theory that all matter and energy in the universe was compressed into an extremely small volume that suddenly, billions of years ago, began expanding in all directions.

Biosphere – The part of the Earth System that includes all living organisms and dead and decaying matter.

Black hole – A hole in space formed by the collapse of a very large supernova. Its gravity is so great that not even light can escape.

Chromosphere – A reddish layer in the middle of the Sun's atmosphere, the transition between the outermost layer of the Sun's atmosphere, or corona, and the photosphere.

Comet – A mass of frozen gases, ice, and rocky debris that orbits the Sun.

Constellation – A pattern of stars in the night sky.

Corona – The outer layer of a star's atmosphere, such as that of the Sun's, extending millions of kilometers, and consisting of gas heated to very high temperatures.

Coronal mass ejections – (CMEs) Gases in the corona of the Sun that break free because they are so hot that the Sun's gravity cannot hold them. The gases form a solar wind.

Cosmologist – A scientist who studies the origin and dynamics of the universe.

Crater – A round depression, or pit-like feature found on the surface of some planets and moons that is formed by the impact of a meteorite. Similarly shaped features can be found on volcanoes and the sites of explosions.

Crust – The outermost layer of the Earth, including the continents and ocean floor. Crust is composed of rock, sediment, and soil, representing less than 0.1% of the Earth's total volume.

Density – A measure of matter calculated as mass divided by volume, expressed as g/cm^3 or g/mL.

Earth System – A term used to describe the Earth as a set of closely interacting systems. Earth has four major subsystems; the geosphere, the atmosphere, the hydrosphere, and the biosphere.

Electromagnetic spectrum – The complete range of wavelengths of radiation that travel through space.

Electron – A subatomic particle with a negative electrical charge.

Galaxy – A very large-scale system that contains a group of star clusters, with hundred of billions of stars.

Gamma rays – Electromagnetic radiation with a wavelength of about 10^{-12}, a shorter wavelength than visible light.

Gas giant – The name given to the first four outer planets: Jupiter, Saturn, Uranus, and Neptune. These large planets are not composed mostly of rocky or solid material, and consist mostly of gaseous matter.

Geosphere – The part of the Earth System that includes the crust, mantle, and inner and outer core.

Giants – Very large, bright stars, that are dimmer than supergiants, and cooler than Main-Sequence Stars.

Gravity – A force that Earth exerts on any body of material on or at the Earth's surface.

Great Observatories – NASA's series of four observatories in space, designed to study the universe over the entire electromagnetic (EM) spectrum, so cosmologists can see the same object in different ways.

Helium – A light, colorless, odorless, nonflammable gaseous element.

Hydrogen – The lightest of all gases and most abundant element in the universe. It is colorless, odorless, and highly flammable.

Hydrosphere – The part of the Earth System that includes all of the planet's water, including oceans, lakes, rivers, ground water, ice, and water vapor.

Infrared radiation – The electromagnetic radiation with wavelengths between about 0.7 μm to 1000 μm. Infrared waves are not visible to the human eye.

Light-year – A unit of measure equal to the distance light travels in one year, 9.46 trillion kilometers (9.46×10^{12} km). Light-years are used to measure the great distances in space.

Lunar cycle – The orbit of the Moon around the Earth. This process takes an average time of 29 days and 12 hours.

Main Asteroid Belt – A band of rocky space debris located close to the orbit of Neptune and including Pluto, the largest of an estimated 30,000 objects.

Main-sequence stars – A star with characteristics that places it within a band running through the middle of the H-R diagram, and includes more than 90% of all stars.

Mantle – The hot fluid zone of the Earth's interior beneath the crust and above the outer core.

Mass – The amount of matter in an object, measured in kilograms.

Meteor – A streak of light in the sky at night that results when a meteoroid hits Earth's atmosphere and melts, vaporizes, or explodes (commonly know as a shooting star).

Meteorite – A meteor that is large enough to survive its passage through Earth's atmosphere and hit the ground.

Meteoroid – Small rocky bodies that revolve around the Sun.

Mid-oceanic ridge – A chain of undersea ridges extending through all of the Earth's ocean basins, and formed from upwelling magma by sea-floor spreading.

Milky Way Galaxy – The galaxy which contains the Sun and our Solar System, and approximately 100 billion stars.

Model – A model is a representation of a process, event, object, or system that is too big, too distant, too small, too unwieldy, or too unsafe to observe or test directly.

Modeling – Modeling is a procedure in which a representation of a process, event, object or system is constructed to investigate a scientific question.

Nebula – A term used to describe an enormous cloud of gas and dust in space. Nebulae are the birthplace of stars.

Nebular theory – The theory that the Sun and the planets condensed out of a spinning cloud of gas and dust.

Neutron star – A very small star formed from the imploded core of a massive star produced by a supernova explosion.

Organisms – Living things with parts that work together as a whole.

Photon – A unit of electromagnetic energy, regarded as a discrete particle having zero mass, no electric charge, and an indefinitely long lifetime.

Photosphere – The visible surface of the Sun, lying just above the uppermost layer of the Sun's interior, and just below the chromosphere.

Prominence – Huge columns of glowing gases rising from hotspots that arc high about the Sun's surface.

Resolution – The process of making an object or sources of light observable.

Solar flares – Giant explosions of gas on the surface of the Sun. These can only be observed using specialized scientific instruments that can detect radiation released during a flare.

Solar fusion – The process by which the Sun creates energy by the nuclear fusion of hydrogen to produce helium.

Solar System – The Sun together with the planets, asteroids, meteors, moons, comets, and all other celestial bodies that orbit the Sun.

Solar wind – A flow of hot charged particles leaving the Sun, some of which can reach the Earth.

Stratosphere – The layer of the atmosphere that extends upward from the troposphere to an altitude of 50 km.

Sunspots – Cool, dark areas of gas within the photosphere that have intense magnetic activity.

Supergiants – Extremely large, very bright, cool stars close to the end of their lives.

Supernova – The death explosion of a massive star whose core has completely burned out. Supernova explosions can temporarily outshine a galaxy.

Terrestrial planet – A small, dense planet similar to Earth that consists mainly of rocky and metallic material. Terrestrial planets include the inner Solar System planets Mercury, Venus, Earth, and Mars.

Ultraviolet radiation – Electromagnetic radiation at wavelengths shorter than the violet end of visible light; with wavelengths ranging from 5 nm to 400 nm.

Vapor – A substance in the gaseous state.

Volume – The amount of space taken up by an object.

Wavelength – The distance between the crests of two waves in succession.

White dwarfs – A relatively dim star that has exhausted most or all of its nuclear fuel and has collapsed to a very small size.

X-rays – electromagnetic radiation with a wavelength of about 10^{-10}, a shorter wavelength than visible light.

The American Geological Institute and Investigating Earth Systems

Imagine more than 500,000 Earth scientists worldwide sharing a common voice, and you've just imagined the mission of the American Geological Institute. Our mission is to raise public awareness of the Earth sciences and the role that they play in mankind's use of natural resources, mitigation of natural hazards, and stewardship of the environment. For more than 50 years, AGI has served the scientists and teachers of its Member Societies and hundreds of associated colleges, universities, and corporations by producing Earth science educational materials, *Geotimes*–a geoscience news magazine, GeoRef–a reference database, and government affairs and public awareness programs.

So many important decisions made every day that affect our lives depend upon an understanding of how our Earth works. That's why AGI created *Investigating Earth Systems*. In your *Investigating Earth Systems* classroom, you'll discover the wonder and importance of Earth science. As you investigate minerals, soil, or oceans — do field work in nearby beaches, parks, or streams, explore how fossils form, understand where your energy resources come from, or find out how to forecast weather — you'll gain a better understanding of Earth science and its importance in your life.

We would like to thank the National Science Foundation and the AGI Foundation Members that have been supportive in bringing Earth science to students. The Chevron Corporation provided the initial leadership grant, with additional contributions from the following AGI Foundation Members: Anadarko Petroleum Corp., The Anschutz Foundation, Baker Hughes Foundation, Barrett Resources Corp., Elizabeth and Stephen Bechtel, Jr. Foundation, BPAmoco Foundation, Burlington Resources Foundation, CGG Americas, Inc., Conoco Inc., Consolidated Natural Gas Foundation, Diamond Offshore Co., Dominion Exploration & Production, Inc., EEX Corp., ExxonMobil Foundation, Global Marine Drilling Co., Halliburton Foundation, Inc., Kerr McGee Foundation, Maxus Energy Corp., Noble Drilling Corp., Occidental Petroleum Charitable Foundation, Parker Drilling Co., Phillips Petroleum Co., Santa Fe Snyder Corp., Schlumberger Foundation, Shell Oil Company Foundation, Southwestern Energy Co., Texaco, Inc., Texas Crude Energy, Inc., Unocal Corp. USX Foundation (Marathon Oil Co.).

We at AGI wish you success in your exploration of the Earth System!

Ann Benbow
Director of Education, AGI

Marcus E. Milling
Executive Director, AGI

Illustrations and Photos

A60 (Left), A61 (Top), A63 (Bottom Left Composite) Anglo-Australian Observatory/David Malin

A5, A6 (Bottom), A12, A22, A23, A24 (Bottom), A39, A40 (Top and Bottom), A41, A46, A53 (Middle and Top), A65 by Stuart Armstrong

Av (Top and Bottom), Axii, A2, A10, A16, A17, A28, A36, A37, A47, A48, illustrations by Dennis Falcon

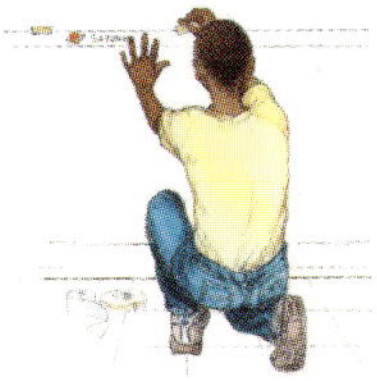

A68 (Top) Fermilab Visual Media Services

A38 Getty Images

Axi (Bottom Right), A68 (Bottom) Griffith Observatory/Anthony Cook

A24 (Top) Tom McGuire

A70 (Top) courtesy of the NAIC - Arecibo Observatory, a facility of the NSF

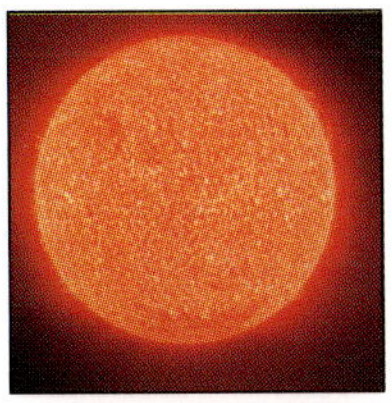

Axi (Top Right and Bottom Left), A4, A5, A6 (Top), A9, A15, A30 (Top and Bottom), A33, A41, A42 (Left), A43 (Top and Bottom), A53 (Bottom), A69, A71 (Top and Bottom), NASA

A66 NASA, Wolfgang Brandner JPL-IPAC, Eva K. Grebel

A60 (Top and Middle), A63 (Top and Bottom Left Composite) NASA/CXX/M. Weiss

A1 NASA Goddard Space Flight Center

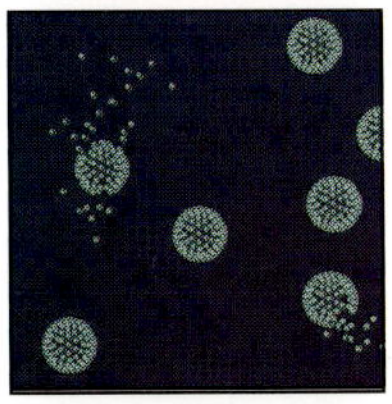

A62 (Middle Left) NASA Headquarters -Greatest Images of NASA (NASA-HQ-GRIN)

A67 NASA, The Hubble Heritage Team

A26, A51 (Right), A70 (Bottom) NASA Jet Propulsion Laboratory (NASA-JPL)

A51 (Bottom) NASA/JPL-Caltech/R. Hurt (SSC-Caltech)

A42 (Top) NASA, Courtesy McRel

A55 NASA, Robert Williams and the Hubble Deep Field Team (STScl)

A64 (Left and Middle) NASA/WMAP Science Team

A8 Courtesy NASCO

Axi (Top Left), A8 (Top), A13, A14, A44, A50, A51 (Top), A52, A57, A60 (Middle), A61 (Bottom), A62 (Top Right, Bottom Left and Right), A73, A74 (Middle) Photodisc

A29 Wojtek Rychlik